JOB
NON   **S**

Books and CD-ROMs by Drs. Ron and Caryl Krann█

The Almanac of International Jobs and Careers
Best Jobs for the 1990s and Into the 21st Century
Change Your Job, Change Your Life
The Complete Guide to International Jobs and Careers
The Complete Guide to Public Employment
The Directory of Federal Jobs and Employers
Discover the Best Jobs for You!
Dynamite Answers to Interview Questions
Dynamite Cover Letters
Dynamite Resumes
Dynamite Salary Negotiations
Dynamite Tele-Search
The Educator's Guide to Alternative Jobs and Careers
Find a Federal Job Fast!
From Air Force Blue to Corporate Gray
From Army Green to Corporate Gray
From Navy Blue to Corporate Gray
High Impact Resumes and Letters
Interview for Success
Job Search Letters That Get Results
Job-Power Source CD-ROM
Jobs and Careers With Nonprofit Organizations
Jobs for People Who Love Computers and the Information Highway
Jobs for People Who Love Health Care and Nursing
Jobs for People Who Love Hotels, Resorts, and Cruise Ships
Jobs for People Who Love to Work From Home
Jobs for People Who Love Travel
Mayors and Managers
Moving Out of Education
Moving Out of Government
The New Network Your Way to Job and Career Success
The Politics of Family Planning Policy
Re-Careering in Turbulent Times
Resumes and Cover Letters for Transitioning Military Personnel
Shopping and Traveling in Exotic Asia
Shopping in Exciting Australia and Papua New Guinea
Shopping in Exotic Places
Shopping the Exotic South Pacific
Treasures and Pleasures of Hong Kong
Treasures and Pleasures of India
Treasures and Pleasures of Indonesia
Treasures and Pleasures of Italy
Treasures and Pleasures of Morocco
Treasures and Pleasures of Paris and the French Riviera
Treasures and Pleasures of Singapore and Malaysia
Treasures and Pleasures of Thailand
Treasures and Pleasures of the Philippines
Ultimate Job Source CD-ROM

JOBS AND CAREERS WITH NONPROFIT ORGANIZATIONS

Profitable Opportunities With Nonprofits

Ronald L. Krannich, Ph.D.
Caryl Rae Krannich, Ph.D.

IMPACT PUBLICATIONS
Manassas Park, VA

JOBS AND CAREERS WITH
NONPROFIT ORGANIZATIONS:
Profitable Opportunities With Nonprofits

Library of Congress Cataloging-in-Publication Data

Krannich, Ronald L.
   Jobs and careers with nonprofit organizations: profitable
opportunities with nonprofits / Ronald L. Krannich, Caryl Rae
Krannich
      p. cm.
   Includes bibliographical references and index.
   ISBN 0-942710-66-5 : $15.95
1. Nonprofit organizations—Vocational guidance—United
States. 2. Associations, institutions, etc.—Vocational guid-
ance—United States. 3. Nonprofit organizations—United
States—Employees. 4. Associations, institutions, etc.—United
States—Employees. I. Krannich, Caryl Rae. II. Title
HD2769.2.U6K7   1996
361.7'02—dc20   95-37801
                                                 CIP

For information on distribution or quantity discount rates, call 703/361-7300
or write to: Sales Department, Impact Publications, 9104-N Manassas Drive,
Manassas Park, VA 22111-5211, Tel. 703/361-7300 or Fax 703/335-9486.
Distributed to the trade by National Book Network, 4720 Boston Way, Suite
A, Lanham, MD 20706, Tel. 301/459-8696.

CONTENTS

NOTE TO USERS

While we have attempted to provide accurate and up-to-date information in this book, please be advised that names, addresses, and phone numbers do change and that organizations do move, go out of business, or change management. This is especially true for organizations located in the New York City and Washington, DC metropolitan areas. Service and program orientations may also change. We regret any inconvenience such changes may cause to your job search.

If you have difficulty contacting a particular organization included in this book, please do one or all of the following:

- Consult the latest edition of *The National Directory of Addresses and Telephone Numbers* (Omnigraphics).

- Contact the Information or Reference section of your local library. They may have online services or directories which include the latest contact information.

- Call Information for current phone numbers.

Inclusion of organizations in this book in no way implies endorsements by the authors or Impact Publications. The information and recommendations are provided solely for your reference. It is the reader's responsibility to take initiative in contacting, evaluating, and following-through with employers.

The names, addresses, phone numbers, and services appearing here provide one important component for conducting a successful job search amongst nonprofit organizations. Placed within the larger context of an effective job search, this component should be carefully linked to your self-assessment, research, networking, and resume writing and distribution activities.

PREFACE

Get ready for a new nonprofit world in the decade ahead. It's likely to be more active, responsive, and effective than ever before. Indeed, the coming decade should be one of the most challenging and exciting periods for nonprofit organizations. As governments at all levels "reinvent" themselves through downsizing and decentralization, many of the social welfare, education, environmental, consumer protection, and entitlement programs that evolved since the 1930s will be significantly modified, if not eliminated altogether. While governments may contract-out some downsized programs to nonprofit organizations, many programs will simply disappear.

Nonprofit organizations play very significant roles at the local, state, regional, and national levels. They represent well defined interests, conduct research, provide direct services, and lobby for legislation. Representing thousands of employers, these organizations especially appeal to individuals who are passionately committed to a cause, enjoy pursuing public issues, and love their work. While you may not get rich working for a nonprofit organization, your life most likely will be forever enriched by the experience.

As both governments and businesses continue to downsize their personnel and programs, nonprofit organizations will most likely grow. Providing new and expanded services, nonprofits will need to hire more competent personnel as well as better mobilize and manage their limited financial resources. Nonprofit jobs that once served as stepping-stones to jobs in government and business will increasingly become important career tracks within the nonprofit world. We expect more and more individuals to pursue long-term and profitable careers with nonprofit organizations.

If many of our predictions come true, we expect nonprofits will increasingly become important employment arenas for job seekers who would normally turn to government or business for career opportunities. Individuals first entering the job market will look to nonprofit organizations for their first job and then advance or change their careers by moving on to other organizations within the nonprofit world. Others who work for government and business will turn to the nonprofit world for new job opportunities or to change careers.

The following pages provide a glimpse into one of today's least understood but most important employment arenas. Standing between government and business, nonprofit organizations offer millions of job opportunities for individuals interested in the type of work performed by these organizations. The first six chapters examine the structure of the nonprofit world as well as outline job search strategies appropriate for these types of organizations. The remaining three chapters provide brief descriptions and contact information on more than 300 nonprofit organizations, including several major nonprofits that primarily operate in the international arena.

Our organizations by no means represent the larger nonprofit world. Instead, we've included organizations as **examples** of the types of employers and information you will likely encounter once you launch your own job search within the nonprofit world.

Throughout this book we recommend several key resources for conducting your own research on nonprofit organizations. We cannot over-emphasize the importance of familiarizing yourself with these resources early in your job search. Indeed, we strongly urge you to visit your local library immediately—within hours of examining this book—to acquaint yourself with many of these resources, especially several recommended directories. Only if you use this book in conjunction with these other resources will you put yourself in the best position to find a nonprofit job that is right for you.

We wish you well as you navigate your job search through the chaotic world of nonprofit organizations. If you follow our tips and use our recommended resources properly, we're confident you can find a profitable job with nonprofits—a truly rewarding one you will really love!

Ron and Caryl Krannich

JOBS AND CAREERS WITH NONPROFIT ORGANIZATIONS

1

JOBS
AND THE
NONPROFIT
SECTOR

*W*here can you find over 700,000 organizations that employ nearly 10 million Americans? Closer to you than you may think. You'll probably find them just down the street or across town.

Largely neglected by job seekers, nonprofit organizations are found everywhere—in neighborhoods and communities across the country as well as abroad. They comprise a huge complex of organizations focusing on some of today's most exciting issues, dealing with many of today's most passionate problems, and representing some of the nation's most powerful interests. Collectively known as the "nonprofit

1

sector," these organizations offer some of today's most rewarding job opportunities. Best of all, they hire hundreds of people each day. Chances are you qualify for a profitable job in nonprofits.

GOING NONPROFIT

So you think you might want to work for a nonprofit organization. But what exactly is a nonprofit organization? How do they differ from government agencies or business firms? What type of work do they do? What types of positions do they offer? What are some of the positives and negatives of working for these organizations? How much do they pay? How secure are nonprofit jobs? Where can I find vacancies? Whom do I contact? How can I best land a job with a nonprofit? Are there profitable careers with nonprofits?

These and many other questions provide a basis for examining the nonprofit employment arena. Operating in both the public and private sectors, this complex of organizations offers thousands of exciting and rewarding job opportunities. While nonprofits mean different things to different people, let's take a brief look at what comprises the nonprofit sector.

THE PUBLIC/PRIVATE NEXUS

Most people have a distorted and dichotomous view of the world of work. At the simplest level, jobs appear to be found in *either* the public or private sector. Working in the public sector usually means being employed with federal, state, or local government agencies; private sector work is normally considered to be employment in business. And business is usually equated with large Fortune 500 corporations—despite the fact that 85 percent of the population is employed by businesses having fewer than 100 employees and nearly 30 million people are self-employed. Conclusions about the state of the economy and the world of work are often shaped by these simplistic "public/private" and "large corporate" views of employment.

The public/private sector distinction misses a great deal of what really goes on in the world of work. The public sector, for example, includes many government corporations that operate like businesses. It also includes political parties and lobbying groups that primarily focus on influencing the conduct of government but which appear to be neither public nor private organizations.

Worst of all, the public/private sector distinction neglects thousands of organizations that employ nearly 10 million people or eight percent of the population—nonprofit organizations. Being both non-governmental and non-business organizations, nonprofit organizations fall outside the purview of most job seekers' lists of potential employers. Except for an occasional scandal—most recently the United Way and the New Era Foundation—or a major fundraising campaign—your local United Way, Red Cross, Salvation Army, or police benevolent organization—most nonprofits tend to have low public profiles. Understandably, organizations that have low public profiles are not well-known among job seekers.

Most nonprofits tend to have low public profiles and thus are not well-known among job seekers.

A WORLD OF OPPORTUNITIES

While nonprofit organizations may have a low profile amongst job seekers, most people are acquainted with these organizations by means of membership or direct contacts. Indeed, you probably belong to two or three such organizations already, or you regularly come into contact with them during the year.

If you belong to a church, for example, your church is most likely operated as a nonprofit organization. If it's a very large church, it will have full-time employees, from custodians and receptionists to word processors, accountants, and computer specialists. It may also be affiliated with a large religious service organization, such as the Catholic Relief Services or Lutheran World Relief, which spends millions of dollars each year on overseas relief, social development, and technical assistance operations.

If you belong to a labor union or a professional association, you participate in a nonprofit organization.

If you donate money to the United Way, Red Cross, or the Salvation Army, you have contact with large nonprofit organizations that provide full-time employment for thousands of individuals.

And if you sponsor a child through Childreach or the Christian Children's Fund or join the American Automobile Association (AAA) the American Association of Retired Persons (AARP), or the National Rifle Association (NRA), you participate in some of the largest and most effective organizations that define the nonprofit world.

Most people think of nonprofit organizations as volunteer and charitable advocacy groups, but savvy job seekers know better. The nonprofit world offers numerous job opportunities for enterprising job seekers. While many such organizations do have volunteer programs, engage in charitable activities, and advocate for a particular cause, they do much more. Many of these organizations operate with large full-time staffs that handle annual budgets in excess of $25 million. Because it is a well-defined employment arena, the nonprofit world has its own employment publications and services. Nonprofits offer a variety of jobs that lead to long-term careers in the nonprofit sector.

Nonprofit organizations offer thousands of exciting and rewarding opportunities.

Whatever you do, don't overlook nonprofit organizations as potential employers. While they may have ʿa low public profile amongst job seekers, they offer thousands of exciting and rewarding opportunities for individuals interested in the type of work performed by nonprofits.

WHAT IS A NONPROFIT?

In strictly legal terms, a nonprofit organization is any organization that has been granted tax exempt status by the Internal Revenue Service. Under Section 501 of the Federal Tax Code, these organizations are granted tax exempt status. According to government regulations, these organizations do not engage in profit-making commercial activities.

However, such a simple, legalistic definition has little to do with day-to-day realities. Some nonprofit organizations do indeed fit this definition, but many other nonprofits engage in profitable commercial activities in order to fund their operations. The U.S. Committee for UNICEF, for example, sells greeting cards. The American Association of Retired Persons (AARP) and National Education Association (NEA) both sponsor profitable travel programs. Similar to many major businesses, many nonprofits pay their top administrators generous salaries, extend nice corporate perks, and house their operations in attractive high-rent commercial buildings. The National Wildlife Foundation, American Automobile Association, and the American Association of Retired Persons, for example, operate very lucrative direct-mail operations, offer special health and life insurance rates, and sponsor profitable educational programs. Subsidized by the U.S. Postal Service—which permits them to use inexpensive nonprofit postal rates for running lucrative direct-mail operations and for mobilizing members to political action—many of these groups ostensibly compete with businesses.

In reality, over 700,000 nonprofit organizations employ nearly 10 million people or approximately eight percent of the total workforce. While many of these organizations consist of only one or two-person volunteers or part-time employees, at least 35,000 nonprofit organizations offer full-time job and career opportunities; more than 5,000 organizations have full-time staffs of ten or more people and operate large volunteer programs. Engaging in a variety of interesting activities, these organizations tackle popular public policy and social welfare issues that make them so appealing to millions of job seekers. Whether they are strictly "nonprofit" is less important than what they actually do on a day-to-day basis.

At the most general level, nonprofit organizations are neither public nor private organizations. Falling between these two groups, nonprofits are non-governmental and non-business organizations that at times behave like government and business organizations. They perform a bewildering array of functions and engage in an amazing range of public activities. Many of these organizations are at the forefront of getting major issues, such as child labor, auto safety, hunger, homelessness, AIDS, civil rights, nuclear power, cancer, and environmental degradation, on governments' policy agendas. Many function as educational groups, foundations, charities, and trade and professional associations.

Perhaps the best way to define nonprofit organizations is to examine their specific activities, primary missions, or public passions. While nonprofit organizations come in many different forms, shapes, sizes, and orientations, most fall into these twelve categories:

1. **Private educational organizations:** Consist of private nonprofit elementary, secondary, and postsecondary educational institutions. Primarily local groups with affiliated national and international alumni.

2. **Religious organizations:** Include a wide range of religious groups, such as churches, synagogues, mosques, and evangelical organizations with small to large membership bases. Comprised of local groups which may be affiliated with larger national and international groups.

3. **Arts, cultural, historical, and community-educational organizations:** Encompass museums, opera companies, symphony orchestras, nonprofit theaters, and libraries. Primarily community-based groups.

4. **Health organizations:** Include hospitals, clinics, nursing homes, and allied health care organizations. Primarily local groups controlled by local boards of notables.

5. **Social service organizations:** Encompass the largest number of nonprofits. These groups provide a wide range of assistance to different population groups, from the homeless, orphans, and battered spouses to the handicapped, elderly, and refugees. Primarily local groups, but many of these organizations also are affiliated with national and international parent organizations. These groups are the stereotypical organizations that define the nonprofit world in many peoples' minds.

6. **Advocacy and political groups:** Include such noted groups as Greenpeace, Common Cause, NAACP, and the Sierra Club. Many are national and international in scope.

Focus on influencing the content of public policy through public education and political action.

7. **Business, professional, and trade/labor organizations:** Promote educational and political support activities for members. Many of these groups or associations border on being for-profit organizations. Some of the best-known such groups include the American Bar Association, American Medical Association, AFL-CIO, National Rifle Association, National Manufacturers Association, and the U.S. Chamber of Commerce. Many are national in scope and include regional, state, and local chapters. Offer excellent job opportunities for individuals skilled in communication and meeting planning.

8. **Scientific and research organizations:** Conduct research and experiments used by government agencies and businesses. Include research and development organizations and think tanks, such as RAND Corporation, American Enterprise Institute, and the Urban Institute.

9. **Community development organizations:** Focus on strengthening communities in the areas of employment, economic development, housing, education, and health care. Primarily local grassroots organizations.

10. **Foundations:** Engage in philanthropic activities that fund many other nonprofit organizations, especially education, art, health, and social service groups. While most are community-based, others such as the Ford Foundation, Rockefeller Foundation, and Johnson Foundation are national and international in scope.

11. **Youth leadership and development organizations:** Consist of groups such as the Cub Scouts, Boy Scouts, Girl Scouts, and Camp Fire Girls and Boys.

12. **Utility companies:** Include cooperative electrical generation and irrigation organizations primarily operating in rural areas and small towns.

While this is a useful classification encompassing nearly 90 percent of all nonprofit organizations, some groups tend to fall into more than one or two categories. For example, many religious organizations also operate educational, social service, and health organizations. Business and professional groups also may sponsor educational and research organizations.

> # *Nonprofit organizations are neither public nor private organizations.*

These twelve types of organizations further break out into several major activity categories with corresponding examples of nonprofit organizations:

Aid to the handicapped

- American Foundation for the Blind
- Federation of the Handicapped
- Goodwill Industries
- National Industries for the Blind
- Paralyzed Veterans of America

Alumni associations

- Associated Students UCLA
- Princeton University Alumni Organization
- Stanford Alumni Association
- University of Virginia Alumni Association

Blood banks

- American Red Cross
- Blood Systems, Inc.
- Oklahoma Blood Institute

Business or professional association

- American Bankers Association
- American Petroleum Institute
- National Association of Home Builders
- U.S. Chamber of Commerce

Care and housing for the aged

- Council for Jewish Elderly
- National Lutheran Home for the Aged
- Methodist Home for the Aged, Inc.

Care and housing of children

- James Barry-Robinson Home for Boys
- Father Flanagans Boys Home

Church groups

- Lutheran Church Missouri Synod Foundation
- Seventh Day Adventists
- United Methodist Church

Civil Rights

- NAACP
- National Urban League
- Southern Christian Leadership Conference

Community Chest, United Fund, etc.

- Heart of America United Fund
- Salvation Army
- United Way of America

Community foundations and trusts

- Chicago Community Trust
- The Columbus Foundation

- Kalamazoo Foundation
- New York Community Trust

Conservation, environmental groups

- Green Peace U.S.A., Inc.
- National Audubon Society
- National Geographic Society
- National Wildlife Federation
- Sierra Club

Credit unions

- Commonwealth Credit Union
- Credit Union National Association, Inc.
- Metropolitan Credit Union
- Telephone Workers Credit Union

Cultural and arts

- The Asia Society
- American Film Institute
- Wolf Trap Foundation for the Performing Arts

Emergency and disaster aid

- American National Red Cross
- Food for the Hungry, Inc.
- World Relief

Evangelism

- Billy Graham Evangelistic Association
- Robert Schuller Ministries, Inc.
- Jimmy Swaggart Ministries

Family planning

- Foster Parents Plan, Inc.
- Planned Parenthood Federation of America

Gifts and grants

- American Institute for Cancer Research
- Amnesty International of U.S.A., Inc.
- Ford Foundation
- Lilly Endowment, Inc.
- RJR Nabisco Foundation
- Save the Children Federation, Inc.

Health insurance and services

- American Academy of Family Physicians
- American Lung Association
- Dr. Martin Luther King Health Center
- Health Insurance Association of America
- Total Health Care

Hospitals

- Good Samaritan Hospital Association, Inc.
- Holy Cross Hospital
- Presbyterian Hospital
- University Hospitals of Cleveland

Housing for the aged

- Episcopal Retirement Homes, Inc.
- Hebrew Home for the Aged
- United Methodist Memorial Home

Libraries

- Brooklyn Public Library
- Online Computer Library Center, Inc.
- Enoch Pratt Free Library of Baltimore City

Museums, zoos, planetariums

- American Museum of Natural History
- Cleveland Museum of Art

- Smithsonian Institution
- Zoological Society of San Diego

Nursing or convalescent home

- Mega Care, Inc.
- Peninsula General Nursing Home
- Scripps Home

Prepaid group health plans

- Blue Cross and Blue Shield
- Group Health Service Plan
- Kaiser Foundation Health Plan, Inc.

Private schools

- Harvard School
- Menninger Foundation
- Phillips Academy

Professional associations

- American Bar Association
- American Medical Association
- National Association of Manufacturers
- National Rifle Association

Radio or television broadcasting

- Christian Broadcasting Network
- National Public Radio
- Trans World Radio

Religious activities

- Aid Association for Lutherans
- Catholic Aid Association
- United Jewish Appeal
- Womens Christian Association

Scholarships

- Culver Education Foundation
- Ford Motor Company Fund
- National Merit Scholarship Corporation
- The Rotary Foundation of Rotary International

School related activities

- African-American Institute
- Close Up Foundation
- Educational Testing Service
- Up With People, Inc.

Schools, colleges, trade schools

- Adelphi University
- Bard College
- Colorado College
- Roosevelt University

Scientific research

- American Cancer Society
- Hudson Institute, Inc.
- Salk Institute for Biological Studies
- Wortham Foundation

Special schools

- Braille Institute of America
- Landmark Foundation
- Perkins School for the Blind

Sponsored research groups

- Petroleum Research Fund
- Rand Corporation
- SRI International

Student loans

- College Foundation, Inc.
- Dartmouth Educational Loan Corporation
- Student Finance Corporation

Utility companies

- Cooke County Electric Cooperative Association
- Mountain Electric Cooperative, Inc.
- Tri-County Electric Cooperative

YMCA and YWCA

- Armed Services YMCA of the U.S.A.
- Young Mens Christian Association of Metropolitan Chicago
- Young Womens Christian Association of Los Angeles

Youth organizations

- American Youth Soccer Organization
- Boy Scouts of America National Council
- Boys Clubs of America
- Girl Scouts of the United States of America
- Little League

Most nonprofits function at the state and local levels. However, many nonprofits also are organized at the international and national levels. Some, such as the United Way and the International Red Cross, have affiliated state and local organizations that operate at the grassroots level.

POSITIONS AND SKILLS SOUGHT

Nonprofit organizations need comptrollers, program officers, meeting planners, accountants, bookkeepers, librarians, office managers, computer specialists, community organizers, education and communication specialists, publicists, researchers, writers, editors, lobbyists, word processors, and mail room personnel along with specialists in particular subject areas. Because nonprofits are heavily dependent upon membership dues, contributions, grants, and direct-mail sells to fund their operations, they highly prize individuals who demonstrate strong communication, public relations, and fundraising skills. If you have strong communication skills, enjoy working with the public, and feel comfortable recruiting members and asking strangers for contributions, you may be an ideal candidate for working with a nonprofit organization!

Nonprofit organizations hire for all types of positions, from chief executive officer to receptionist.

The types of jobs and skills required for nonprofit organizations will vary with the type and size of nonprofit organization. **Private educational organizations**, for example, disproportionately hire elementary, secondary, and postsecondary teachers and administrators, similar to those in the public sector. On the other hand, **museums, opera companies, symphony orchestras, and theaters** hire talented curators, artists, production personnel, actors, and stage hands as well as both full-time and part-time administrative staff disproportionately engaged in communication and fundraising activities. **Social service organizations** hire numerous professionals who provide counseling and development services. **Advocacy and political groups** hire a disproportionate number of public policy specialists, researchers, writers, and community activists. **Business and professional organizations** seek communication specialists, researchers, writers, meeting planners, publicists, and lobbyists. **Scientific and research organizations** disproportionately hire subject specialists with demonstrated research and writing skills as well as librarians. **Foundations** need program officers, researchers, and librarians.

Regardless of the type and size of organization, most nonprofits need individuals with strong communication and fundraising skills, because they must constantly mobilize public support for their activities. Indeed, individuals with limited work experience, but who can demonstrate strong communication skills, can organize and manage well, show a willingness to engage in critical fundraising activities, and are enthusiastic and eager to get things done are in a strong position to land an entry-level position with a nonprofit organization.

CHOOSE THE RIGHT RESOURCES

We wish you well as you pursue a job or career in the nonprofit sector. In the following chapters we primarily survey major nonprofit employers. Many other job search issues, especially key job search steps we allude to in Chapter 4, are outlined in our other books: *Change Your Job Change Your Life, Discover the Best Jobs for You, High Impact Resumes and Letters, Dynamite Resumes, Dynamite Cover Letters, Dynamite Tele-Search, Job Search Letters That Get Results, Interview for Success, Dynamite Answers to Interview Questions, The New Network Your Way to Job and Career Success*, and *Dynamite Salary Negotiations*. We also address particular jobs and career fields in the following books: *The Complete Guide to Public Employment, The Directory of Federal Jobs and Employers, Find a Federal Job Fast, The Complete Guide to International Jobs and Careers, The Almanac of International Jobs and Careers, The Educators Guide to Alternative Jobs and Careers, Best Jobs for the 1990s and Into the 21st Century*, and *Jobs for People Who Love Travel*. While available in many bookstores and libraries, these and many other job search books also are available directly from Impact Publications. For your convenience, you can order them by completing the order form at the end of this book or by acquiring a copy of their catalog.

Contact Impact Publications to receive a free copy of the most comprehensive career catalog available today—*"Jobs and Careers for the 1990s."* For the latest edition of this catalog of hundreds of annotated job and career resources, write to:

IMPACT PUBLICATIONS
ATTN: Job/Career Catalog
9104-N Manassas Drive
Manassas Park, VA 22111-5211

They will send you a copy upon request. This catalog contains almost every important career and job finding resource available today, including many titles that are difficult, if not impossible, to find in bookstores and libraries. You will find everything from self-assessment books to books on resume writing, interviewing, government and international jobs, military, women, minorities, students, and entrepreneurs as well as videos, audiocassettes, and computer software programs. This excellent publication will help you keep in touch with the major resources that can assist you with every stage of your job search as well as with your future career development plans.

EMPOWER YOURSELF IN THE NONPROFIT WORLD

The chapters that follow should help empower you for the wonderful world of nonprofit organizations. If you follow our tips and are persistent in making key contacts and following-up, you'll discover a large complex of organizations involved with all types of interesting and challenging issues and representing important interests. In many respects the nonprofit world is an organizational jungle, but it's one you should be able to easily untangle. You must take a great deal of initiative to make sense of that portion of the nonprofit world that most appeals to your interests, values, and skills.

We wish you well as you put this book into practical use. The remaining chapters are designed to introduce you to the nonprofit employment world. Take the time to explore some of our many recommended resources which are readily available at your local library. Better still, during the next week, introduce yourself to some nonprofit organizations by making a few phone calls for information, advice, and referrals. You may be surprised what you learn. You'll discover the nonprofit world is much closer than you think. And it may just have the perfect job for you. If you do this, you'll understand why so many other people love what they are doing in the nonprofit sector. They have a job that's "fit" for them!

2

MYTHS,
REALITIES,
& CURRENT
TRENDS

*I*f you're not familiar with nonprofit organizations, you may try to approach them like you would any other type of organization. Nonprofits differ from government and business organizations in many ways. They have their own particular financial and support structures as well as employment and work cultures which you should attempt to understand before approaching them for job opportunities.

Let's take a look at the nature of these organizations by way of some popular myths, realities, and current trends.

18

MYTHS AND REALITIES

Numerous myths relate to the nonprofit sector. Unfortunately, many of these myths dissuade job seekers from exploring opportunities with nonprofit organizations. We've found ten myths to be some of the most common ones discouraging individuals from seeking job and career opportunities with nonprofits:

MYTH 1: **Nonprofits offer few job opportunities.**

REALITY: Employing nearly 10 million people, nonprofits serve as employers for nearly eight percent of the American workforce. While many nonprofits are very small and only employ one or two full-time people, many other nonprofits employ over 100 individuals. Many job seekers overlook nonprofits as sources for employment not because they offer few job opportunities but, rather, because they know little about these organizations.

MYTH 2: **It's difficult to find information on opportunities with nonprofit organizations.**

REALITY: In addition to this book, you will find many useful printed resources on opportunities with nonprofit organizations published by Barricade Books, Gale Research, Planning/Communication, and The Taft Group. You also will find similar information online through the commercial online services, such as America Online and CompuServe, as well as on the Internet.

MYTH 3: **Nonprofits are primarily volunteer organizations involved in charitable activities.**

REALITY: Many nonprofit organizations depend on volunteers, but many of these same organizations have large full-time paid staffs. It is inappropriate to stereotype nonprofit organizations as charitable organizations made up of volunteers. Nonprofits consist of a wide range of different types of organizations, from educational groups to foundations. Volunteers play important roles in only some types of nonprofit organizations.

MYTH 4: **Nonprofits lack good entrepreneurial skills and a sense of productivity and accountability. Like government employees, they are used to drawing salaries unrelated to performance.**

REALITY: By definition, nonprofits must be entrepreneurial, productive, and accountable. Their funding operations require recruiting members, acquiring donations, receiving grants, and operating profit-making commercial enterprises. Indeed, they must be entrepreneurial in order to raise sufficient funds to survive and grow. Like most government and business organizations, they work within annual budgets. Similar to large businesses, many nonprofits must advertise their activities. However, nonprofit entrepreneurism differs from private sector entrepreneurism. Non-profit entrepreneurism centers on fundraising activities rather than on the marketing and selling of products or services. Nonprofits also must be productive and accountable in relation to board members who set policies, approve budgets, and oversee operations. Nonprofit productivity is measured differently from business productivity. Similar to government productivity, nonprofit productivity is measured in reference to organizational goals.

MYTH 5: **Nonprofit organizations are primarily located in the metropolitan areas of Washington, DC, New York, Chicago, and Atlanta.**

REALITY: Many of the large nonprofits, which are national and international in scope, are headquartered in these major metropolitan areas. The organizations have large full-time staffs which offer excellent job opportunities leading to career advancement within the nonprofit sector. However, more than 90 percent of all nonprofits operate at the local level as community-based organizations. While these groups have smaller staffs and fewer positions than the large nonprofits headquartered in major metropolitan areas, nonetheless, the local nonprofits generate millions of job opportunities.

MYTH 6: **It's difficult to break into the nonprofit world.**

REALITY: It can be easier to enter this employment arena than to find jobs in government or business. Many nonprofits offer entry-level volunteer and internship positions through which individuals can acquire experience and skills with nonprofit organizations.

MYTH 7: **Most nonprofits are liberal groups that hire do-gooder, social-action types.**

REALITY: While many nonprofits attract individuals with such political and social orientations—especially liberal social advocacy groups—many other nonprofits attract conservatives and those who do not have social action agendas. Nonprofits fall all along the ideological spectrum, from liberal environmental and abortion rights groups to conservative religious right and pro-life groups. Both types of groups attract individuals who have a passion for taking action related to a particular social issue. Other groups, such as professional associations, are relatively apolitical as they seek to promote the collective interests of their members. Nonprofits need accountants, fundraisers, researchers, writers, communication specialists, administrators, and managers who have the necessary skills to develop organizations and maintain day-to-day operations.

MYTH 8:   **Nonprofit jobs tend to be deadend jobs.**

REALITY: This is a huge employment arena where many individuals develop long-term careers and report high levels of satisfaction. Career advancement often takes the track of moving from small to larger nonprofit organizations that offer increasing responsibilities and operate larger budgets.

MYTH 9:   **Nonprofit organizations offer low salaries and few benefits.**

REALITY: The level of pay and benefits can vary widely, depending on the nature of the nonprofit organization. It's true that many nonprofit organizations, especially charitable and social service organizations, offer low-paying jobs because of the volunteer nature of the work and their shoestring budgets. But many nonprofits, especially health groups, research organizations, foundations, and business and professional associations, offer excellent salaries and benefits.

MYTH 10:   **The best way to find a job with a nonprofit organization is to respond to vacancy announcements in local newspapers.**

REALITY: Many positions are advertised in local newspapers. However, many more jobs are found through direct application and through electronic databases. Groups such as Access, which publish job listings with nonprofits in the monthly *Community Jobs*, even announces job vacancies electronically through America Online. For a comprehensive review of hundreds of international, national, state, and local job vacancy resources, see the latest edition of Dan Lauber's *The Nonprofit's Job Finder* (Planning/Communications).

POSITIVES AND NEGATIVES

What's it really like working in the nonprofit sector? Most people either know little or nothing about nonprofit work, or they have certain stereotypes about what it's really like working in this employment arena. Reality depends on the type of organization, where you work, and whom you work with. In general, however, the following positives and negatives are normally associated with nonprofit organizations. Some are two-edged swords—they function as both positives and negatives.

Nonprofits enable many people to pursue their passions in well-focused work environments.

Positives

1. **Rewarding work:** Many nonprofit organizations have a positive impact on the health and welfare of people. They do "good works" that are compatible with the religious and social values of individuals who want to help others and become involved in improving their communities. People who seek meaningful work find nonprofits provide an excellent job "fit". They enable many people to pursue their passions in well-focused work environments.

2. **Interesting and exciting work:** Much of the work of nonprofits is very interesting and exciting. Arts, cultural, historical, community-educational, social service, advocacy,

political, and business and professional organizations engage in some of today's most important work. Many of their missions center on pressing social and political issues. If you want to change the attitudes and behaviors of individuals, groups, and communities, you'll find many nonprofits to be ideal employers.

3. **Positive work environments:** Some of the nicest, most caring, and selfless people you will ever meet work for nonprofit organizations. Many of these organizations also hire very bright and well-educated individuals who contribute to an intelligent and stimulating work environment. If you like working with such people—and especially those who share your values and are very likable—a nonprofit organization may be the right type of environment for you.

4. **Easy entry and valuable experience:** Nonprofits offer excellent opportunities for acquiring working experience. Indeed, it is often easier to acquire entry-level positions with nonprofit organizations than with government agencies and businesses. Indeed, nonprofits offer a large number of volunteer and internship experiences for acquiring work experience. Recent college graduates and women re-entering the workforce often find nonprofit organizations to be more responsive to their job search initiatives than government agencies and businesses.

5. **Career advancement:** Many nonprofit jobs lead to career advancement within the nonprofit sector. This often involves moving from small to larger nonprofit organizations. Nonprofits also are excellent stepping stones for acquiring jobs in government and business. Indeed, many people working in government and business today first acquired work experience with nonprofit organizations.

Negatives

1. **Low pay:** Constrained by limited financial resources, many nonprofit organizations offer below average to low salaries. Comparable jobs paying $30,000 a year in

government or business may only pay $22,000 with a nonprofit organization. A 25 percent salary differential is quite common. Consequently, don't expect to make as much money working for a nonprofit organization as you might with other types of organizations. The rewards are elsewhere, and primarily non-monetary, with nonprofits.

2. **Limited career advancement:** Since many nonprofits are small organizations, your career within such an organization may quickly plateau. Career advancement requires leaving a small nonprofit organization for a higher level job in a larger nonprofit organization. However, many of the larger nonprofits are found in only a few major metropolitan areas such as Washington, DC, New York, Philadelphia, Boston, Atlanta, Chicago, Minneapolis, Denver, San Francisco, and Los Angeles. If you are unwilling to seek employment with larger nonprofits headquartered in these cities, don't expect to advance your career much in the nonprofit sector.

3. **Stressful and frustrating work environments:** Work environments of many nonprofit organizations leave much to be desired. Many are stressful because of the chaotic nature of their organizations and decision-making. Many nonprofits are highly political and bureaucratic. Boards of directors often work against their best interests. Some nonprofits have notorious reputations for administrative incompetence and disorganization; lack quality personnel and staff development; and operate with antiquated equipment and from cramped quarters. Relationships between the CEO, board members, staff, and volunteers can become a nightmare. If you prize strong leadership, clear decision points, and high levels of efficiency, many nonprofit organizations will disappoint, frustrate, and discourage you. If you can tolerate ambiguity, inefficiency, and chaos, you may do well in such work environments.

4. **Lack of concrete results and accountability:** While many nonprofits promote positive social values, many of these organizations are hard-pressed to point to concrete

measurable results to justify their operations. Unlike a business that measures its performance by its bottomline profits, few nonprofits have similar types of performance indicators. They operate *processes* which may or may not be directly related to specific performance and outcomes. Many of these processes involve frequent meetings and reports—but few outcomes. Like government agencies, nonprofit organizations have annual budgets which they must expend.

5. **Uncertain financial future:** By definition most nonprofits depend on a variety of fundraising activities, from membership fees and public donations to foundation grants and government contracts. Fluctuating from year to year, such unpredictable funding levels can create anxiety amongst employees, generate job insecurity, and affect motivation.

CURRENT TRENDS

Recent trends appear to be supportive of a greater role for nonprofit organizations. Indeed, we see the continuing increase, expansion, and strengthening of nonprofits in the decade ahead. Six trends in particular lead us to this conclusion:

1. **Nonprofits are taking on more "public" responsibilities as governments continue to downsize and divest themselves of certain social welfare and community development functions.** The watershed congressional elections of November 1994 signaled a significant shift in how government will do business in the decade ahead. Numerous programs which used to receive generous federal, state, and local government support—from education and social welfare to museums, libraries, and public radio and television—are now experiencing major cuts in their annual government-supported budgets. As a result, more and more of these organizations will need to "reinvent" themselves in order to survive and prosper. The successful ones will conduct very aggressive public relations and fundraising campaigns which will require the hiring of more talented personnel skilled in these crucial organiza-

tional development functions. As governments continue to downsize and divest themselves of traditional social welfare functions, more and more nonprofit organizations, especially charities, will play an increasingly important role in providing welfare assistance. Functioning as new and expanded service delivery organizations, they will increase their professional staffs to provide such services as well as secure increased funding through government contracts and grants. In the international arena, NGOs (non-governmental organizations) will play a more important role in international development and relief efforts as the U.S. Agency for International Development and the United Nations undergo further budgetary cuts.

2. **Funding activities continue to increase despite recessions and occasional scandals.** Americans continue to support and use nonprofits at unprecedented levels. They view nonprofits as more responsive and accountable than government bureaucracies. Since many nonprofits are community-based, they also seem to be more democratic and participatory than government. As governments divest themselves of certain educational, cultural, health, and welfare functions as well as downsize many entitlement programs, nonprofit organizations should receive increased financial support from government. While occasional scandals, such as the recent United Way and New Era Foundation episodes, will likely continue in the future, they will not substantially affect public commitment to supporting nonprofit organizations.

3. **Nonprofits will become more entrepreneurial.** Whether they like it or not, nonprofits are businesses that require sound technical, managerial, communication, marketing, and sales talent in order to survive and prosper in today's highly competitive public environments. Many of these organizations are underfunded and lack strong administrative capabilities. They need more and more creative self-starters who can move these organizations into the 21st century on sound financial, technical, and managerial bases.

4.   **Nonprofits will continue to offer excellent employment opportunities in the decade ahead.** As nonprofits grow, they will continue to expand as attractive employment arenas. Best of all, they are major players in the revolving door of government and business. Many people who work for government eventually leave for jobs with nonprofit organizations. Many who work in business also leave to work for nonprofits. It's not unusual to find individual career paths beginning in government, moving on to nonprofit organizations, and then going on to corporations. Experience with nonprofit organizations can be an important stepping-stone to exciting career opportunities in both government and business.

5.   **Nonprofits will continue to include numerous types of organizations, many of which will be controversial.** While most nonprofits are stereotyped as charitable organizations, in reality they represent a very diverse set of organizations. Expect to see more and more nonprofit organizations, especially advocacy groups, come under closer government scrutiny because of their political and commercial activities. Some of these organizations may lose their nonprofit status.

6.   **Jobs with nonprofit organizations will increasingly become more technical in nature.** Today's fast-paced and highly competitive nonprofit world requires individuals who have adequate technical skills to operate effective high-tech organizations. This means being proficient in using the latest computer software programs and online electronic services as well as communicating via e-mail.

These and other trends continue to change the complexion of this fascinating employment arena. Neither public nor private, nonprofit organizations offer some terrific job and career opportunities for those who understand where they are coming from and where they are going in the decade ahead.

3

EXAMINE
YOUR
NONPROFIT
CAPABILITIES

*D*o you have the right skills, motivations, and attitudes to do well in today's nonprofit job market? Maybe you do, maybe you don't, or perhaps you need to take certain actions that will enhance your ability to do well in the nonprofit sector.

Not everyone is a good candidate for the work of nonprofit organizations. Take a look at your potential level of success in the nonprofit sector by completing the exercise on pages 30-32.

29

YOUR NSL (Nonprofit Success Level) QUOTIENT

Respond to each of the following statements by circling which number at the right best represents your situation.

SCALE: 1 = strongly agree   4 = disagree
            2 = agree   5 = strongly disagree
            3 = maybe, not certain

1. I enjoy working with people who
    need assistance.   1   2   3   4   5

2. I work well with different types of
    people and in diverse work settings.   1   2   3   4   5

3. I'm a self-starter who takes initiative
    in pursuing new ideas and solving
    problems.   1   2   3   4   5

4. I work well without close supervision.   1   2   3   4   5

5. I'm enthusiastic about my work.   1   2   3   4   5

6. I can influence others to do things
    my way.   1   2   3   4   5

7. I'm more interested in the type of
    work I'm doing and the people I'm
    working with than in the amount of
    money I'm making.   1   2   3   4   5

8. I'm tolerant of other peoples' views
    and generally empathize with others.   1   2   3   4   5

9. I'm more interested in providing
    public services and helping others
    than in making money.   1   2   3   4   5

10. I can handle ambiguity and complexity
    in my daily work.   1   2   3   4   5

11. I'm tolerant of most organizational
    politics.   1   2   3   4   5

12. I can work well in loosely structured environments and can tolerate a certain degree of on-going disorganization. 1 2 3 4 5

13. I'm flexible in the way I deal with people, processes, and problems. 1 2 3 4 5

14. I enjoy working in environments where consensus building is important to decision making. 1 2 3 4 5

15. I'm tolerant of relatively chaotic work environments that may lack leadership, quick and decisive decision-making, and strong administrative processes. 1 2 3 4 5

16. I'm a team player who does not require strong leadership for direction. 1 2 3 4 5

17. I'm not interested in having a big office and acquiring organizational perks normally associated with large businesses. 1 2 3 4 5

18. I'm willing to accept a lower salary for a job I really love. 1 2 3 4 5

19. I enjoy working in small organizations. 1 2 3 4 5

20. I'm willing to engage in fundraising activities. 1 2 3 4 5

21. I'm a committed advocate who is interested in persuading others to support my views. 1 2 3 4 5

22. I'm looking for meaningful work that involves associating with people who have similar interests and goals. 1 2 3 4 5

23. I'm not a "get rich quick" type of person; I'm more interested in the work I'm doing than in making money. 1 2 3 4 5

24. I'm willing to accept a job that
offers limited career advancement.   1 2 3 4 5

25. I'm willing to learn and grow a
career in the nonprofit sector.   1 2 3 4 5

26. I have strong written and oral
communication skills.   1 2 3 4 5

27. I don't mind making cold calls and
asking strangers for information and
assistance.   1 2 3 4 5

28. I know where to find vacancy
information on jobs with nonprofit
organizations.   1 2 3 4 5

29. I have a resume designed specifically
for nonprofit organizations.   1 2 3 4 5

30. I know at least three people who work
with nonprofit organizations, who are
willing to talk to me about their
work, and who will provide me with
information, advice, and referrals.   1 2 3 4 5

31. I can present myself well at a
job interview.   1 2 3 4 5

32. I know the types of questions an
interviewer is likely to ask me
at an interview for a nonprofit job.   1 2 3 4 5

33. I know how to find information on
specific nonprofit organizations,
including the salaries and benefits
they offer.   1 2 3 4 5

34. I know at least five nonprofit organizations that hire individuals with
my interests, skills, and abilities.   1 2 3 4 5

TOTAL   _____

INTERPRET YOUR SCORE

Although there is no scientific validation to correlate one's responses on this NSL questionnaire to one's success working for a nonprofit, you can get an indication of your *potential for success* by adding the numbers you circled to get an overall composite score. If your total is more than 100, you may not be a good candidate at present for a job with many nonprofit organizations. You may need to work on improving your knowledge, skills, abilities, and attitudes in relation to each item for which you circled a 3, 4, or 5. If your overall score is under 60, congratulations; you are probably a good candidate for success in the nonprofit sector!

4

EFFECTIVE JOB SEARCH STRATEGIES & TECHNIQUES

*F*inding a job with a nonprofit organization is similar to finding a job with many other types of organizations. You first need to understand how the nonprofit job market is structured and then focus on where to find job vacancies, how to uncover job leads, and how to best communicate your qualifications to employers. To be most effective, you need to develop job search strategies and techniques that are particularly responsive to nonprofit organizations.

9 STEPS TO JOB SEARCH SUCCESS

Conducting an effective job search with a nonprofit organization should include the following steps:

1. **Decide what it is you do well and enjoy doing in reference to nonprofit organizations.** It's always best to begin any job search by conducting a thorough self-assessment of your interests, skills, and abilities. You can do this by taking different examinations, such as the popular *Myers-Briggs Type Indicator* or the *Strong Interest Inventory,* which are readily available through professional career counselors, testing centers, or counseling centers of community colleges. Alternatively, you may want to complete a variety of self-directed exercises which can also yield valuable information on your interests, skills, and abilities. We've included many of these exercises in our other book, *Discover the Best Jobs for You.*

> *Will the position be a good "fit" for you or might it be "unfit" for your particular mix of interests, skills, and abilities?*

The real value in doing this up-front self-assessment work is knowing how suitable you will be for particular positions with nonprofit organizations. These tests and exercises will help you identify your pattern of motivated abilities—those things you really do well and enjoy doing. Once you identify a potential employer and a specific position, you want to know if you have the right combination of interests, skills, and abilities to do the job. In other words, will the position be a good "fit" for you or might it be "unfit" for your particular mix of interests, skills, and abilities? If you fail to do this, you could well end up with a job that is not fit for you, one which leads to unhappiness and disappointments for both you and the employer. This self-assessment will also help you identify an appropriate language with which to write your resumes and letters as well as talk about your interests, skills, and abilities with employers.

Make sure your goals are <u>employer-centered</u> rather than self-centered.

---

2. **State a clear objective of what it is you really want to do if and when you become employed by a nonprofit organization.** Employers are especially receptive toward hiring individuals who have a clear idea of what they want to do. They especially like individuals whose goals coincide with their specific needs. Job applicants with clear objectives tend to write well-crafted resumes and letters as well as communicate confidence and enthusiasm during interviews—two characteristics employers seek in candidates. Employees, in turn, tend to most enjoy their work when it coincides with their expectations and goals. Be sure to identify what it is you really want to do in reference to employers' needs. Make sure your goals are **employer-centered** rather than self-centered. For example, a typical self-centered goal might be this:

> "An increasingly responsible management position that leads to career advancement with a large nonprofit organization."

While this may represent a personally honest objective, it does not impress an employer as much as this employer-centered objective:

"A management position with responsibility for building a strong membership base that will more than double contributions within the next three years."

This objective clearly speaks to the specific needs of many nonprofit employers. If you fail to develop an objective, you may appear unfocused and thus organize your job search in a very disorganized manner.

3. **Conduct research on appropriate nonprofit organizations, employers, and positions.** Knowledge is power when looking for a job. Without research you will lack power in the nonprofit job world. Unfortunately, few applicants really do their homework to learn about the job market, organizations, employers, and specific positions suitable for their particular interests, skills, and abilities. They send resumes and go to interviews knowing little or nothing about the employer's needs. Worst of all, they get to the salary negotiation stage uninformed about current salary ranges for comparable positions. Fortunately, there is a wealth of information available on nonprofit organizations, and it's readily available to anyone with a minimum amount of effort—a trip to the library or a phone call, fax, or e-mail message. Most major libraries include directories to nonprofit organizations, such as the *National Directory of Nonprofit Organizations* (The Taft Group), *Encyclopedia of Associations* (Gale Research), *Good Works* (Barricade Books), *Finding a Job in the Nonprofit Sector* (The Taft Group), and *The Almanac of International Jobs and Careers* (Impact Publications). These directories provide names, addresses, and telephone and fax numbers as well as annotated descriptions on thousands of nonprofit organizations. They are good starting points for identifying nonprofit organizations that most appeal to you given your interests, skills, and motivations. For comparable salary information, consult *Compensation in Nonprofit Organizations* (Abbott, Langer, and Associates). Other useful resources help identify job vacancies: *The Nonprofit's Job Finder* (Planning/Communication), *Community Jobs: The National Employment Newspaper for the Non-Profit Sector* (212/475-1001) and

The Chronicle of Philanthropy (800/347-6969). Many professional groups and associations, such as The Taft Group, U.S. Chamber of Commerce, American Society of Association Executives, and the Society for Nonprofit Organizations, maintain databases on nonprofit organizations as well as provide job assistance to members. But your best resource will be you, yourself, talking with individuals who are knowledgeable about the nonprofit sector. Talk to people who are involved with nonprofit organizations, from board members to full-time staff and volunteers; who know what it's really like working for organizations X, Y, and Z; and who can give you useful information, advice, and contacts. The point here is that you need both knowledge and realistic expectations about your future employer. You can gain invaluable information by conducting library research and by interviewing people who are knowledgeable about your areas of concern. If you neglect to do such research—spend at least two to three weeks gathering useful information before applying for jobs—you will neglect one of the most important phases of getting a job. If done properly, your research will reveal a wealth of useful information that will help you target your job search on specific employers. Best of all, your research will help you identify organizations, employers, and positions you should avoid as well as actively seek out.

Employers want to know what it is you have done, can do, and will do for them.

4. **Write dynamite resumes and letters that grab the attention of individuals interested in your experience.** Your single most important calling card for nonprofit employers will be your resume. It says who you are and what you can likely do for them. Always write your resume

with the needs of employers in mind. They want to know what it is you have done, can do, and will do for them. They look for experience and **patterns of accomplishments** that may be directly relevant to their operations. Since employers are busy people who have limited time to digest a lengthy resume, keep your resume to one or two pages—the shorter and more succinct the better. You may want to write two types of resumes—conventional and electronic. The conventional resume is designed to be read by hiring personnel. Electronic resumes are designed to be electronically scanned. The principles for writing such resumes, including examples of effective resumes and letters, are found in our *Dynamite Resumes* and *High Impact Resumes and Letters* and in Peter Weddle's *Electronic Resumes for the New Job Market* as well as on pages 74-88 of Chapter 6 of this book.

Many jobs with nonprofits are never advertised.

---

5. **Conduct informational interviews and network for information, advice, and referrals.** While current job listings are a convenient way of identifying job vacancies, one of the best ways to find quality jobs is through network-ing. Indeed, many jobs with nonprofits are never advertised. Thousands of jobs are found and filled through informal means—word-of-mouth, friends, family, and the ubiquitous "connection." Therefore, you are well advised to plug into the informal word-of-mouth communication channels by initiating a well-organized networking campaign designed for yielding quality information, advice, and referrals. At the heart of this networking process is the informational inter-view. Conducted over the telephone or in face-to-face settings, the informational interview helps you penetrate the unadvertised job market where many quality jobs will be found. Focused on individuals who are well-positioned to

give useful information, advice, and referrals, the informational interview can yield an enormous amount of information that can be critical to the overall direction of your job search. Details on the informational interview, including sample dialogues, appear in two of our other books, *The New Network Your Way to Job and Career Success* and *Interview for Success*. See pages 69-71 for examples.

6. **Target specific organizations and employers.** It is always preferable to target specific organizations and employers rather than cast a very broad and unfocused net. When you target your job search, you focus only on those organizations and employers that have jobs appropriate for your interests and skills. Targeting enables you to focus your attention on a manageable number of employers. For example, rather than broadcast your resume and cover letter to 1000 nonprofit organizations, identify 20 key organizations you would like to work for. Devote at least five hours to learning about each organization. Spend another five hours on each organization networking for information, advice, and referrals; developing presentation packages and delivering them to the appropriate hiring personnel; and following up with letters, phone calls, faxes, and e-mail. You'll quickly discover that job search success comes from understanding the hiring details of each organization and persisting in working those details to your advantage. Above all, it requires persistence in following-through with information, advice, and referrals acquired through your networking activities.

7. **Write lots of letters, make numerous phone calls, and learn to communicate effectively by fax and e-mail.** Communication, communication, communication lies at the heart of any successful job search, and written communication plays an even more important role today given the widespread use of faxes and e-mail systems. Effective communication takes many different forms and mediums. Remember, you are a stranger to most hiring personnel in nonprofit organizations. Your job is to persuade them to notice you as well as take your candidacy seriously. Above all, you must communicate your qualifications loud and

clear—and error free—to strangers who have the power to hire. You need to convince them that you have the requisite skills and talent to make a positive contribution to their operations. You also need to project a positive personality—you are a thoughtful and likable person who will get along well with others in the organization. But how do you do this? Which communication mediums appear to be most effective with hiring personnel? You initially communicate these qualities in letters as well as over the telephone and in faxes and e-mail. You will need to write a variety of letters—which also can be converted into faxes and e-mail messages—throughout your job search—cover, approach, resume, follow-up, and thank-you. One of the most effective letters you can write is the thank-you letter. Make sure you follow-up with such letters. They say a lot about you as an individual—qualities hiring personnel look for when screening candidates. For a comprehensive treatment of such letters, including writing principles and examples, see our *Dynamite Cover Letters* and *Job Search Letters That Get Results: 201 Great Examples*. Also, make sure you use the telephone, fax machine, and e-mail systems. Busy people have difficulty responding to letters and telephone messages. If you send a letter of inquiry or a cover letter and resume, be sure to follow-up with a telephone call, fax, or e-mail within five working days. In fact, many people now prefer receiving faxes or e-mail rather than telephone calls because fax and e-mail messages are easier to sort, respond to, and control. Given the widespread use of voice mail systems, many telephone calls get recorded rather than received by a real person. Since busy people are often confronted with 20 or more voice mail messages each day, it's virtually impossible for them to return all of their calls. If they did, they would have little time for other pressing work. On the other hand, a well-crafted fax or e-mail message may be more effective in getting a response from the person. Faxes and e-mail get the immediate attention of recipients who feel obligated to respond to what appears to be time-sensitive communication. Our advice for today's rapidly changing communication mediums: become a good fax and e-mail communicator! For information on the use of telephones, faxes, and e-mail systems in your job search, see our *Dynamite Tele-Search: 101 Telephone Techniques and Tips for Getting Job Leads and Interviews*.

If you send a letter, be sure to follow-up with a telephone call, fax, or e-mail within five working days.

---

8. **Develop effective interview and salary negotiation skills and schedule job interviews.** The most critical step in landing a job is the actual job interview. You must take initiative in order to get job interviews. This requires regularly following-up your job search communication and scheduling job interviews. Be prepared for different types of interviews, from the telephone screening interview to panel and stress interviews. The best way to prepare is to anticipate the types of questions you are likely to be asked about your goals, education, experience, and personality. Outline answers to such questions with both positive form and content. For example, can you give very positive answers to these questions? *"Tell me about yourself"* and *"Why should we hire you?"* Can you talk intelligently about your goals in reference to the employer's needs as well as discuss relevant accomplishments in previous jobs? If you can't, or if you are uncertain, now is the time to prepare for such questions. At the same time, you should be prepared to ask intelligent questions. Indeed, the quality of your questions may be just as important to landing the job as the quality of your answers to the interviewer's questions. In the job interview, you simply won't have a second chance to make a good first impression! And that's what the job interview is all about—making good impressions verbally and nonverbally. For details on how to handle the critical job interview, see

our *Dynamite Answers to Interview Questions* and *Interview for Success* as well as Richard Fein's *101 Dynamite Questions You Should Ask At the Job Interview* (Impact Publications).

You constantly want to be remembered as someone who should be called for a job interview.

---

9. **Follow-up, follow-up, follow-up.** The weakest link in the job search tends to be the follow-up process. Many people write terrific resumes and letters and are good at networking for information, advice, and referrals. But they fall down at the stage where everything must come together—follow-up. You simply must develop an effective follow-up campaign if you expect get attention and positive responses to your job search initiatives. Assume that most hiring personnel are busy people who have little time to take your candidacy seriously. The one thing you can do that will separate you from the pack of other applicants is to engage in certain follow-up activities that will get results. At the very minimum, you should follow-up all written and mailed communication with a telephone call. If you sent a cover letter and resume, call within five working days to inquire if the individual received your materials and ask when you might expect to hear from them. Follow-up that follow-up call with a nice thank-you letter for taking the time to speak with you and reiterate your interest in the position. If you don't hear within another two weeks, make a similar telephone call reiterating your interest in the position and asking again when you might anticipate hearing from them. The key to effective follow-up activities is to keep your name and application active in the mind of the recipient without

becoming a pushy, annoying pest. You constantly want to be **remembered** as someone who should be called for a job interview. Therefore, your follow-up calls must project you as someone who is interested, friendly, enthusiastic, and competent. And remember, every time you initiate a telephone follow-up, you're probably engaging yourself in a telephone interview. So be prepared to respond to potential telephone screening interview questions.

20 PRINCIPLES FOR SUCCESS

The principles for job search success with nonprofit organizations are the same as those for success with most other types of organizations.

Success is determined by more than just a good plan getting implemented. We also know success is not determined primarily by intelligence, time management, or luck. Based upon experience, theory, research, common sense, and acceptance of some self-transformation principles, we believe you will achieve job search success by following many of the following 20 principles:

1. **You should work hard at finding a job with a nonprofit organization:** Make this a daily endeavor and involve your family.

2. **You should not be discouraged with set-backs:** You are playing the odds, so expect disappointments and handle them in stride. You will get many "no's" before finding the one "yes" which is right for you.

3. **You should be patient and persevere:** Expect three to six months of hard work before you connect with the job that's right for you.

4. **You should be honest with yourself and others:** Honesty is always the best policy. But don't be naive and stupid by broadcasting your negatives and shortcomings to others.

5. **You should develop a positive attitude toward yourself:** Nobody wants to employ guilt-ridden people with inferiori-

ty complexes. Focus on your positive characteristics—not your negatives.

6. **You should associate with positive and successful people:** Finding a job largely depends on how well you relate to others. Avoid associating with negative and depressing people who complain and have a "you-can't-do-it" attitude. Run with winners who have a positive "can-do" outlook on life.

7. **You should set goals:** You should have a clear idea of what you want and where you are going. Without these, you will present a confusing and indecisive image to others. Clear goals help direct your job search into productive channels. Moreover, setting high goals will help make you work hard in getting what you want.

8. **You should plan:** Convert your goals into action steps that are organized as short, intermediate, and long-range plans.

9. **You should get organized:** Translate your plans into activities, targets, names, addresses, telephone numbers, and materials. Develop an efficient and effective filing system and use a large calendar to set time targets, record appointments, and compile useful information.

10. **You should be a good communicator:** Take stock of your oral, written, and nonverbal communication skills. How well do you communicate? Since your job search involves communicating with others—and communication skills are one of the most sought-after skills—always present yourself well both verbally and nonverbally.

11. **You should be energetic and enthusiastic:** Employers are attracted to positive people. They don't like negative and depressing people who toil at their work. Generate enthusiasm both verbally and nonverbally. Check on your telephone voice—it may be more unenthusiastic than your voice in face-to-face situations.

12. **You should ask questions:** Your best information comes from asking questions. Learn to develop intelligent questions that are non-aggressive, polite, and interesting to others. But don't ask too many questions and thereby become a bore.

13. **You should be a good listener:** Being a good listener is often more important than being a good questioner or talker. Learn to improve your face-to-face listening behavior (nonverbal cues) as well as remember and use information gained from others. Make others feel they enjoyed talking with you, i.e., you are one of the few people who actually *listens* to what they say.

14. **You should be polite, courteous, and thoughtful:** Treat gatekeepers, especially receptionists and secretaries, like human beings. Avoid being aggressive or too assertive. Try to be polite, courteous, and gracious. Your social graces are being observed. Remember to send thank you letters—a very thoughtful thing to do in a job search. Even if rejected, thank employers for the "opportunity" given to you. After all, they may later have additional opportunities, and they will remember you.

15. **You should be tactful:** Watch what you say to others about other people and your background. Don't be a gossip, back-stabber, or confessor.

16. **You should maintain a professional stance:** Be neat in what you do and wear, and speak with the confidence, authority, and maturity of a professional.

17. **You should demonstrate your intelligence and competence:** Present yourself as someone who gets things done and achieves results—a *producer*. Employers generally seek people who are bright, hard working, responsible, communicate well, have positive personalities, maintain good interpersonal relations, are likable, observe dress and social codes, take initiative, are talented, possess expertise in particular areas, use good judgment, are cooperative,

trustworthy, and loyal, generate confidence and credibility, and are conventional. In other words, they like people who score in the "excellent" to "outstanding" categories of the annual performance evaluation.

18. **You should not overdo your job search:** Don't engage in overkill and bore everyone with your "job search" stories. Achieve balance in everything you do. Occasionally take a few days off to do nothing related to your job search. Develop a system of incentives and rewards—such as two non-job search days a week, if you accomplish targets A, B, C, and D.

19. **You should be open-minded and keep an eye open for "luck":** Too much planning can blind you to unexpected and fruitful opportunities. You should welcome serendipity. Learn to re-evaluate your goals and strategies. Seize new opportunities if they appear appropriate.

20. **You should evaluate your progress and adjust:** Take two hours once every two weeks and evaluate what you are doing and accomplishing. If necessary, tinker with your plans and reorganize your activities and priorities. Don't become too routinized and thereby kill creativity and innovation.

These principles should provide you with an initial orientation for starting your job search. As you become more experienced, you will develop your own set of operating principles that should work for you in particular employment situations.

THINGS TO DO IF
YOU LACK EXPERIENCE

Nonprofit organizations provide numerous entry-level opportunities for individuals without work experience. If you are graduating from college with little or no work experience or re-entering the job market after a lengthy absence, nonprofit organizations may offer some ideal job opportunities for you. This is not to say that nonprofits disproportionately hire the inexperienced or unskilled. Rather, given the nature of their organizations, they offer numerous opportunities to acquire work experience which may not be available with other types of organizations. If you are inexperienced, we recommend doing the following:

1. **Be willing to volunteer your services, acquire an internship, or work part-time.** Many nonprofit organizations consist of four major employment groups: board members, volunteers, part-time staff, and full-time staff. Many also offer internship opportunities. In some organizations, especially charitable, the number of volunteer positions may outnumber the full-time staff positions. An excellent way to gain experience is to acquire a volunteer position or an internship. When you contact a nonprofit organization, be sure to ask if they have a volunteer program, volunteer positions, internships, or part-time positions. You may discover that while the organization is not hiring at present for full-time positions, it does have a very active volunteer program. Many volunteers later move on to full-time staff positions with nonprofit organizations. Indeed, volunteering not only gives you invaluable experience, but this experience also will help you decide if nonprofit organizations are the right employers for you. With a minimum investment of your time, you may learn this employment arena is not really for you.

2. **Always demonstrate your enthusiasm, energy, and competence.** Employers like individuals who are enthusiastic and energetic self-starters. Better still, they like those who demonstrate their competence in solving problems, taking initiative, and operating well with a limited amount of supervision. You can make up for your lack of experience by communicating these qualities to employers. They are the qualities of individuals who can learn and grow within organizations.

3. **Apply for as many jobs as possible.** There's a big nonprofit world out there with hundreds of job opportunities for which you probably qualify. While it is always preferable to target your job search on a few employers, individuals with

little or no relevant work experience first need to land a job in order to acquire experience. Therefore, try to apply for as many jobs as possible in order to learn about nonprofit employers and to get experience interviewing for nonprofit jobs. While you may end up with a job that may not be a perfect "fit," it is a job nonetheless. And a job will give you experience for refining your goals.

ORGANIZE AND SEQUENCE YOUR JOB SEARCH

While we recommend that you plan your job search, we also caution you to avoid the excesses of too much planning. Planning should not be all-consuming. Planning makes sense because it focuses attention and directs action toward specific goals and targets. It requires you to set goals and develop strategies for achieving the goals. However, too much planning can blind you to unexpected occurrences and opportunities—that wonderful experience called serendipity. Given the nature of the job market, you want to do just enough planning so you will be in a position to take advantage of what will inevitably be unexpected occurrences and opportunities arising from your planned job search activities. Therefore, as you plan your job search, be sure you are flexible enough to take advantage of new opportunities.

Based on our previous discussion of the sequence of job search steps, we outline on page 50 a hypothetical plan for conducting an effective job search. This plan incorporates the individual job search activities over a six-month period. If you phase in the first five job search steps during the initial three to four weeks and continue the final four steps in subsequent weeks and months, you should begin receiving job offers within two to three months after initiating your job search. Interviews and job offers can come anytime—often unexpectedly—as you conduct your job search. An average time is three months, but it can occur within a week or take as long as five months. If you plan, prepare, and persist at the job search, the pay-off will be job interviews and offers.

While three months may seem a long time, you can shorten your job search time by increasing the frequency of your individual job search activities. If you are job hunting on a full-time basis, you may be able to cut your job search time in half. But don't expect to get a

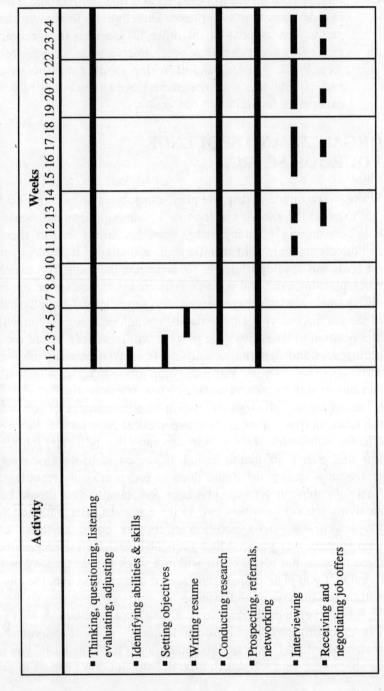

ORGANIZATION OF JOB SEARCH ACTIVITIES

job—especially a job that's right for you—within a week or two. Job hunting requires time and hard work—perhaps the hardest work you will ever do—but if done properly, it pays off with a job that is right for you.

TAKE RISKS AND HANDLE REJECTIONS

You can approach a job or career change in various ways. Some actions have higher pay-offs than others. Many people waste time by doing nothing, reconstructing the past, worrying about the future, and thinking about what they should have done. This negative approach impedes rather than advances careers.

A second approach is to do what most people do when looking for a job. They examine classified ads, respond to vacancy announcements, and complete applications in personnel offices. While this approach is better than doing nothing, it is relatively inefficient as well as ineffective. You compete with many others who are using the same approach. Furthermore, the vacancy announcements do not represent the true number of job vacancies nor do they offer the best opportunities. You should use this approach to some degree, but it should not preoccupy your time. Responding to vacancy announcements is a game of chance, and the odds are usually against you. It makes you too dependent upon others to give you a job.

The third approach to finding a nonprofit job requires *taking creative action* on your part. You must become a self-reliant risk-taker. You identify what it is you want to do, what you have acquired skills to do, and organize yourself accordingly by following the methods outlined in this chapter. You don't need to spend much time with classified ads, employment agencies, and personnel offices. And you don't need to worry about your future. You take charge of your future by initiating a job search which pays off with job offers. Your major investment is *time*. Your major risk is being turned down or rejected.

Job hunting is an ego-involving activity. You place your past, abilities, and self-image before strangers who don't know who you are or what you can do. Being rejected or having someone say "no" to you will probably be your greatest job hunting difficulty. We know most people can handle two or three "no's" before they get discouraged. If you approach your job search from a less ego-involved perspective, you can take "no's" in stride; they are a normal aspect of your job search experience. Be prepared to encounter 10, 20, or 50 "no's." Remember, the odds are in your favor. For every 20 "no's" you get, you also should uncover one or two "yeses." The more rejections you get, the more acceptances you also will get. Therefore, you must encounter rejection *before* you get acceptances.

This third approach is the approach we recommend for finding a profitable job with nonprofits. Experience with thousands of clients shows that the most successful job seekers are those who develop a high degree of self-reliance, maintain a positive self-image, and are willing to risk being rejected time after time without becoming discouraged. This approach will work for you if you follow our advice on how to become a self-reliant risk-taker in today's job market. Better yet, if you use networking strategies, you can significantly decrease the number of "no's" you receive on your way to a nonprofit job that's right for you!

5

RESOURCES TO HELP YOU LAND THE RIGHT JOB

*W*here exactly should you begin your job search? Should you look in the classified sections of newspapers or trade publications for job listings? Is there a central clearinghouse for nonprofit job vacancy information? What about professional associations? Do they offer placement services, operate job banks, or advertise vacancies? Are there online job services? Would you be better off contacting a nonprofit organization directly for information on job opportunities?

53

ORGANIZATIONAL AND JOB VACANCY INFORMATION

A wealth of information is readily available on job opportunities with nonprofit organizations. Indeed, once you discover how to access this information, you may be overwhelmed with having to sort through so many alternatives!

You can easily access information on nonprofit organizations and job vacancies in your local library, over the telephone, or by using a computer. If you buy only one book on nonprofit organizations, we strongly suggest acquiring the latest edition of Daniel Lauber's *Non-Profits' Job Finder* (Planning/Communications). This book is literally a directory to all the major job listing sources relevant to nonprofit organizations. Organized by occupational areas and states, this comprehensive and affordable resource includes newspapers, trade journals, job banks, and online services available at the local, state, and national levels. If you can't find any appropriate job vacancies relevant to your skills and experience through this directory, chances are none are available. Lauber's book should function as a companion directory to this book. His book is available in most libraries and in many bookstores, or it can be ordered directly from Impact Publications by completing the order form at the end of this book.

KEY DIRECTORIES

Any job search relating to nonprofit organizations should begin with the following directories. Most are readily available in major libraries:

> *Compensation in Nonprofit Organizations* (Crete, IL: Abbott, Langer & Associates, Tel. 708/672-4200). An annual survey of salaries for over 40,000 positions (87 job categories) in more than 2,000 nonprofit organizations.

> *Encyclopedia of Associations* (Detroit, MI: Gale Research). One of the most useful directories for researching nonprofit organizations. This four-volume annual directory annotates nearly 25,000 associations. Provides a wealth of information on each organization: name, address, phone and fax number, name of primary officials, founding date, staff size, number of members,

activities, budget information, official publications, and regional, state, and local groups. Includes useful geographic and executive indexes. Most libraries routinely carry the newest annual edition which is published in July of each year. Many libraries also have the CD-ROM version of this directory which helps in quickly sorting information for targeting specific nonprofit associations. Additional volumes also include regional, state, and local associations and international associations. An annual supplement is published in November of each year.

Encyclopedia of Medical Organizations and Agencies (Detroit, MI: Gale Research). Provides information on more than 12,000 public and private organizations and agencies concerned with medical information, funding, research, education, planning, advocacy, advice, and services. Includes names, addresses, telephone/fax numbers, key officials, number of employees and members, and publications.

Finding a Job in the Nonprofit Sector (Washington, DC: The Taft Group, 1991). Somewhat dated and with no plans for a future updated edition, nonetheless, this directory to nonprofit employers is still useful. Profiles nearly 1,000 nonprofit organizations. Many listings include name, address, phone number, activity, and range of annual income. Coverage of individual organizations is often spotty and income data is mostly useless given the large ranges specified for each organization. Includes a few introductory essays. Entries organized alphabetically. Includes two useful indexes—activity and state.

The Foundation Directory (New York: The Foundation Center). This annual directory provides summary information on over 6,300 foundations with assets of at least $2 million or annually disperse $200,000+ in grants. Each entry includes name, address, phone/fax number, assets, support activities, orientation, and key officers. Includes useful geographic and subject indexes. This is the "bible" of the foundation industry.

Good Works: A Guide to Careers in Social Change, Donna Colvin, ed. (New York: Barricade Books, 1994). The newest edition of this unique directory profiles over 1,000 nonprofit organizations dealing with issues of social change. Each entry includes name, address, phone number, purpose, issues/projects, operations, publications, funding sources, contact person, budget, staff numbers, salaries, and vacancy information. Indexed by state and activity.

National Directory of Addresses and Telephone Numbers (Detroit, MI: Omnigraphics). One of our favorite resources, here's the ultimate telephone directory for job seekers. Published annually, this massive telephone/fax directory includes more than 136,000 listings which are organized alphabetically and arranged by subject for different types of businesses and organizations. Includes hundreds of nonprofit organizations along with listings of businesses and industries nationwide. Major nonprofit categories include:

- Alcoholism and Drug Abuse Treatment Centers
- Associations and Organizations
- Blood Banks
- Colleges and Universities
- Credit Unions
- Foundations
- Hospitals
- Libraries
- Museums and Art Galleries
- Political Action Committees
- Political Parties
- Research Organizations and Services

It's well worth spending some time examining various listings for ideas. This unique directory will be available on CD-ROM in 1996.

National Directory of Nonprofit Organizations (Washington, DC: The Taft Group). Published biannually, this three-volume directory is the "bible" for locating thousands of nonprofit organizations. Using the classification system and data available through the Internal Revenue System, the directory lists each organization alphabetically. The first two volumes include all nonprofits with annual income exceeding $100,000. The third volume focuses on nonprofits with annual incomes between $25,000 and $99,000. Each listing includes the name, address, annual income, IRS classification, and whether or not contributions to the organization are tax deductible. The directory also classifies the organizations by two useful indexes—activity and geography. For example, it categorizes all nonprofits whose primary mission is dealing with AIDS, child care, employee benefits, grants, health planning, loans to students, peace issues, veterans affairs, and several other activity areas. If, for example, you are only interested in working for an emergency service organization in the state of Florida, this directory will help you pinpoint specific nonprofits.

National Trade and Professional Associations (Washington, DC: Columbia Books). Published annually, this popular directory looks like a mini-version of the *Encyclopedia of Associations*. Includes addresses, phone/fax numbers, incomes, and employees of nearly 7,500 trade and professional associations. Useful indexes classify organizations by activities, budget size, and geographic location. Available in most libraries.

Research Centers Directory (Detroit, MI: Gale Research). Published biannually, this two-volume directory provides annotated descriptions on over 13,000 nonprofit research units in all fields. Groups entries into 17 chapters that cover five broad subject categories.

Directory of Executive Recruiters (Fitzsimmon, NH: Kennedy Publications). This annual directory is the indispensable guide to executive recruiters, many of whom recruit for major nonprofit organizations. Includes names, addresses, and telephone/fax numbers of 4,100 offices of 2,890 firms in the U.S., Canada, and Mexico.

Job Hotlines USA (Harleysville, PA: Career Communications, Inc., 1995). Latest edition includes over 2,000 job hotlines nationwide—those hard-to-find telephone numbers that lead to recorded job vacancy and application information on a large variety of organizations. Major nonprofit organizations include education, health/medical, and utilities. If you're interested in vacancies with hospitals, this directory is a goldmine of job hotline numbers with such organizations. Listings organized alphabetically and by state and industry. Each entry includes a main address and telephone number along with a highlighted job hotline number.

Most categories of nonprofit organizations have their own organizational directories. For example, if you're interested in nonprofit environmental organizations, you should examine the *Gale Environmental Sourcebook* and the *Environmental Information Directory*, both published by Gale Research. If you are interested in minority organizations, consult *Minority Organizations* (Garrett Park Press) and a series of minority directories produced by Gale Research: *Asian Americans Information Directory*, *Black American's Information Directory*, *Hispanic Americans Information Directory*, and *Native Americans Information Directory*. For women's organizations, consult two directories also published by Gale Research: *Women's Information Directory* and *Encyclopedia of Women's Associations Worldwide*. A good resource for locating these and other relevant directories is the latest edition of Bernard Klein's *The Directory of Directories* (West Nyack, NY: Todd Publications).

ASSOCIATIONS

Several associations provide job information and assistance for individuals interested in nonprofit organizations. Examples of some major such associations related to various categories of nonprofits include:

American Association of Museums
1225 Eye St., NW, Suite 200
Washington, DC 20005
Tel. 202/289-1818

American Association of University Women
1111 16th Street, NW
Washington, DC 20036
Tel. 202/785-7700

American Federation of Teachers
555 New Jersey Avenue NW
Washington, DC 20001
Tel. 202/879-4400

American Hospital Association
1 N. Franklin, Suite 27
Chicago, IL 60606
Tel. 312/422-3000

American Library Association
500 E. Huron Street
Chicago, IL 60611
Tel. 312/944-6780

American Public Health Association
1015 15th Street NW
Washington, DC 20005
Tel. 202/789-5600

American Society of Association Executives
1575 Eye Street NW
Washington, DC 20005
Tel. 202/626-2742

Council On Foundations
1828 L Street NW, Suite 300
Washington, DC 20036
Tel. 202/466-6512

National Association of Social Workers
750 1st Street NE, Suite 700
Washington, DC 20002-4241
Tel. 202/408-8600

National Council of Nonprofit Organizations
1001 Connecticut Avenue NW, Suite 900
Washington, DC 20036
Tel. 202/833-5740

**National Congress for Community
  Economic Development**
1875 Connecticut Avenue NW, Suite 524
Washington, DC 20009
Tel. 202/234-5009

National Committee On Planned Giving
310 Alabama Street, Suite 210
Indianapolis, IN 46204
Tel. 317/269-6274

National Education Association
1201 16th Street NW
Washington, DC 20036
Tel. 202/833-4000

National Society of Fund Raising Executives
1101 King Street, Suite 700
Alexandria, VA 22314
Tel. 703/684-0410

Nonprofit Management Association
315 W. 9th Street, Suite 1100
Los Angeles, CA 90015
Tel. 213/623-7080

Points of Light Foundation
1737 H Street NW
Washington, DC 20006
202/223-9186

Society for Nonprofit Organizations
6314 Odana Road, Suite 1
Madison, WI 3719
Tel. 608/274-9777

U.S. Chamber of Commerce
1615 H Street NW
Washington, DC 20062
Tel. 202/659-6000

Numerous other professional associations maintain in-house job banks, operate placement services, and list jobs in trade publications and newsletters. The major such associations are identified in Chapter 8.

VACANCY ANNOUNCEMENTS

Since most nonprofits are very small community-based organizations, many of them will run classified ads or display ads for job openings in the employment section of newspapers. Therefore, it may be worth monitoring this section of your local newspaper.

Nonprofits which are national in scope advertise many of their professional positions in major newspapers, such as the *Washington Post, New York Times, Chicago Tribune,* or *The Los Angeles Times,* especially in the Sunday editions.

Several newspapers specialize in job listings for nonprofit organizations. The major such newspapers include:

Association Trends (Association Trends, 7910 Woodmont Avenue, #1150, Bethesda, MD 20814-3062, Tel. 301/652-8666). This weekly newspaper is one of the major sources of employment information on associations. It includes numerous job listings in each issue. It also maintains a job referral service. Individuals can take out classified ads announcing their availability for positions. Send $95 for 50 issues.

The Chronicle of Philanthropy (P.O. Box 1989, Marion, OH 43304, Tel. 800/347-6969). Includes 60 to 90 job listings in each biweekly issue for all types of professional nonprofit positions. Send $36 for a 12-issue subscription or $67.50 for a 24-issue annual subscription.

Community Jobs: The Employment Newspaper for the Non-Profit Sector (Access: Networking in the Public Interest, 30 Irving Place, 9th Floor, New York, NY 10003, Tel. 212/475-1001). A "must" resource for anyone looking for a job with nonprofits. Each issue of this 40-page monthly newspaper is filled with informative articles, job hunting tips, and nearly 400 job listings for individuals interested in working in the nonprofit sector. Individuals can subscribe by sending $29 for 3 issues or $39 for 6 issues. The articles and job listings also are available online through AccessPoint (see page 63). Access also publishes an annual *Nonprofit Employers Directory* which includes all nonprofit employers who advertised in *Community Jobs* during the previous twelve months. This publication is available directly from Access by sending $42.50 (includes shipping).

Chronicle of Higher Education (1255 23rd St. NW, Suite 700, Washington, DC 20036, Tel. 202/466-1000). This weekly newspaper includes informative articles on higher education as well as hundreds of classified ads for recruiting university administrators and faculty as well as professional positions with associations and foundations. Send $75.00 for an annual subscription (48 issues) or $3.25 per issue.

National Business Employment Weekly (P.O. Box 435, Chicopee, MA 01021-0435, Tel. 800/562-4868). This weekly newspaper includes hundreds of classified and display ads for all types of positions. The first and third issue of each month includes a special section with 40 or more ads for professionals in the nonprofit sector. Send $3.95 for a single issue, $35 for 8 issues, or $199 for an annual subscription.

The NonProfit Times (Davis Information Group, 190 Tamarack Cr., Skillman, NJ 08558, Tel. 609/921-1251). This monthly publication includes 20-30 job listings in its "National NonProfit Employment Marketplace" for numerous types of nonprofit positions. Send $49 for an annual subscription.

IN-HOUSE JOB SERVICES

Several organizations offer a variety of career services for individuals interested in working in the nonprofit sector. These range from job banks and placement programs to electronic online services. Many nonprofit organizations—such as the American Society of Association Executives, American Public Health Association, National Organization of Women, National Association of Broadcasters, Catalyst, U.S. Chamber of Commerce, Urban Coalition, and the American Chemical Society—operate their own in-house career and placement services. Be sure to check with various nonprofit organizations to see if they maintain a job bank or offer career services.

ONLINE SERVICES

One of the newest online services specifically designed for the nonprofit job market is called **AccessPoint**. Developed by Access—the publisher of the monthly *Community Jobs*—this service is available through American Online by entering the keyword Access.Point. Known as the "AccessPoint Civic Involvement System and Nonprofits Professional Network," AccessPoint operates as both an information network and career center. You will be able to access informative articles as well as job listings through this service. If you do not have access to America Online, contact AccessPoint directly. They will send you a one-month free trial kit for America Online: AccessPoint, 30 Irving Place, 9th Floor, New York, NY 10003, Tel. 212/475-1001.

Several career services are now available through commercial online services, such as CompuServe, Prodigy, and America Online, and on the World Wide Web and the Internet. For a good overview of job and career services available online, see Joyce Lain Kennedy's two books on this subject—*Electronic Job Search Revolution* (Wiley, 1995) and *Hook Up, Get Hired* (Wiley, 1995); James Gonyea's *The On-Line Job Search Companion* (McGraw-Hill, 1994); and Fred Jandt's and Mary Nemnick's *Using the Internet in Your Job Search* (JIST Works, 1995). Since several new career services come online each month, information in these books tends to be quickly dated. Consequently, you'll have to do your own online research to discover what's currently available and appropriate for you. Many of the online career services include job listings with nonprofit organizations.

ELECTRONIC JOB BANKS

You may also want to join an electronic job finding service. Most of these groups have membership fees. Individuals submit an electronic resume which is then scanned into the company's database. Employers contact the company to search for candidates that match their hiring criteria. Nonprofit employers are increasingly using these services to screen candidates. The major such job banks include the following:

Job Bank USA: 1420 Spring Hill Road, Suite 480, McLean, VA 22102, Tel. 800/291-1USA or fax 703/847-1494. This is the nation's premier database company. Call for information on current enrollment fees which will probably run about $125 per year. Enrollees receive a "Career Fitness Kit" which includes several valuable resources, from books to computer software, on organizing an effective job search. Information also available through CareerWeb, a new online service available on the World Wide Web (http://www.careerweb.com).

University Pronet: 3803 E. Bayshore Dr., Suite 150, Palo Alto, CA 94303, Tel. 415/691-1600. Designed for graduates of participating colleges and universities. Call for information on eligibility and fees.

Connexion®: Peterson's Connexion® Services, 202 Carnegie Center, Princeton, NJ 08543-2123, Tel. 800/338-3282, Ext. 561 or Fax 609/243-9150. Designed for currently enrolled full-time students but others can enroll too. Accessed on CompuServe. Call for information on eligibility and fees.

Career Placement Registry: Career Placement Registry, Inc., 302 Swann Avenue, Alexandria, VA 22301, Tel. 800/368-3093 or 703/683-1085. Includes over 110,000 employers in its database. Call for details.

E-Span Job Search: 8440 Woodfield Crossing, Suite 170, Indianapolis, IN 46240, Tel. 800/682-2901. Individuals submit resumes through e-mail on the Internet or through CompuServe. Call for details.

EXECUTIVE SEARCH
FIRMS AND RESOURCES

Many nonprofit organizations recruit their top talent through professional associations and executive search firms. If you seek an executive-level position, you should join as well as contact the American Society of Association Executives (1575 Eye St., NW, Washington, DC 20005, Tel. 202/626-2723). This organization provides in-house career services. It also maintains one of the best libraries on nonprofit organizations—a terrific resource for job hunters.

We also recommend getting a copy of the latest edition of *The Directory of Executive Recruiters* (Kennedy Publications). This is a "bible" for anyone interested in contacting executive recruiters. Many of the firms listed in this directory recruit executive-level professionals for key positions in trade and professional associations as well as in other nonprofit organizations.

The Search Bulletin (The Beacon Group, P.O. Box 641A, Great Falls, VA 22066, Tel. 703/759-4900) is a 25-30 page biweekly newsletter listing 160-200 executive-level positions in the $50,000-$250,000+ range. It includes some listings for nonprofit organizations. Subscriptions are available at the following rates: 6 issues for $140.00; 12 issues for $210.00.

THE ACCESS NETWORK

The single best source of information on job opportunities with nonprofit organizations is Access: Networking in the Public Interest. In addition to publishing a monthly newspaper with informative articles and job listings and managing the AccessPoint online service (see pages 61-62), Access offers additional job and career services: workshops, resume bank, regional newsletters, and executive search. Since Access is in the process of expanding its operations, you may want to call them to find out what services they provide at present. At the very least, you should subscribe to their monthly newspaper, *Community Jobs*. You can contact them at 30 Irving Place, 9th Floor, New York, NY 10003, Tel. 212/475-1001. Access will be moving many of its operations to a new Washington, DC office which will open in late 1995. In the meantime, contact the New York office for information.

Individuals interested in working with international nonprofit organizations should review the specialized resources identified in Chapter 9.

6

NONPROFIT EMPLOYERS AND YOUR JOB SEARCH

*W*ith over 700,000 nonprofit organizations generating nearly 10 million jobs, it's virtually impossible to provide complete or representative coverage of nonprofit employers. Nor is it necessarily desirable for you and others interested in finding a nonprofit job to have such a definitive guide to nonprofit employers. Indeed, such a book would be unwieldy and confined to the reference section of only a few libraries. It would probably consist of several volumes running thousands and thousands of pages—and would still be incomplete!

And if we only examined the largest nonprofits, we would disproportionately cover hospitals, credit unions, educational institutions, and utility companies—organizations which may be of little interest to most people who want to pursue a nonprofit career with different types of organizations, many of which are small to medium in size and which are advocacy, charitable, or philanthropic groups.

OUR CHOICES

Our coverage of nonprofit organizations follows a very simple principle—we chose to profile those organizations which we thought would be of greatest interest to our readers. In this sense, our choices are somewhat arbitrary and follow the stereotypes of many types of nonprofits—organizations that have social agendas, that deal with interesting and important public issues, and whose operations are primarily national or international in scope. These are the types of organizations many individuals get passionate about. We also include several professional associations and international nonprofits, because they offer excellent opportunities for individuals pursuing other types of nonprofit interests and causes. Although there are exceptions, most nonprofits we've listed employ 10 or more people and have budgets of at least $500,000.

Our omissions are obvious and quite intentional. This means we cover few local nonprofits. Furthermore, we skip most hospitals, credit unions, educational institutions, and utility companies. While ostensibly nonprofits, for all intents and purposes, these organizations are large businesses that adhere to special provisions of the Federal Tax Code (Sections 501 c and d) that allow them to financially operate as nonprofits. While they deal with many interesting public issues, these organizations have less discernible social and political agendas.

By excluding most small local nonprofits and including professional associations and international nonprofits, the nonprofit organizations which are profiled in the remainder of this book are primarily located in Washington, DC, New York City, Chicago, and San Francisco. While these cities are the major centers for national and international nonprofit organizations, they by no means represent the overall geographic dispersion of nonprofits. Again, nonprofit organizations are found in every community. Larger communities will have a larger number of nonprofits, reflecting the overall diversity and complexity of such communities.

A STARTER KIT

Most of the nonprofit organizations identified in this book should give you a glimpse into the employment world of nonprofit organizations. You may find four or five organizations of particular interest to you and thus you follow-through by contacting the organizations for more information on employment opportunities. You may even go so far as to find a job with one of the organizations. If you do, that's great; you will have exceeded our expectations. In most cases, however, we expect users to examine our listings for ideas and as a starting place to network for finding a job with particular types of organizations. For example, if you are especially interested in working for an environmental group, you'll find we include information on only 40 nonprofit employers focused on environmental issues. Use these 40 listings as your starting point for exploring these and many other related environmental organizations. Treat our organizations as only the tip of the iceberg—you'll want to also look at the *Gale Environmental Sourcebook, Environmental Information Directory, Encyclopedia of Associations,* and the *National Directory of Nonprofit Organizations* (see Chapter 5) for information on hundreds of additional nonprofit organizations dealing with environmental issues. The same principle applies to all of our other listings—these should be starting points for heading you in the right direction in finding your own suitable nonprofit employer. In this sense, the remainder of the book should become your starter kit for further learning, exploration, and discovery. If you approach the listings in this manner, you will find the right path to a nonprofit organization that is right for you. The result should be a good "fit".

INITIATE CONTACTS
AND FOLLOW-UP

As we noted in Chapter 4, your job search should follow a certain sequence and be based on key principles for success. Assuming you know what you want to do, you have conducted preliminary research, have written a dynamite resume, and understand where to find various job listings, your next step is to make direct contact with potential employers. Once you identify an employer you wish to contact, the first thing you should do is to verify the address and contact person. The best way to do this is to literally pick up the telephone and call for information and advice. In the process, you should try to get other important employment information. Projecting an upbeat, cheery, and enthusiastic voice (you're an assertive but very likable person), your conversation should go something like this:

OPENER: *Hi, this is Marcia Taylor. I need some information on your organization.* (The response is likely to be, what type of information can I help you with?)

CONTACT: *Whom should I contact about potential job openings in your organization?* (Assuming you get a name of a person, go to the next question.)

Could you please transfer me to him? Thanks.

REQUEST: *Hi, this is Marcia Taylor. I'm in the process of gathering information on jobs with environmental organizations. How do you go about hiring for positions in your organization? Do you normally advertise in the local newspaper or a particular trade journal or do you maintain a resume bank?* (Assuming the answer is both, go on to the next question.)

Are you doing any hiring at present?

For what types of positions? Full-time, part-time, volunteer?

How often do vacancies normally occur?

Could I send you a copy of my resume? I'm really interested in your organization and would love to have an opportunity to interview for a position.

ADDRESS: *Should I send my resume directly to you? Are you still located at: _____?*

REFERRAL: *Since you're not hiring at present, do you know any other environmental groups that might be hiring now or perhaps in the near future?*

CLOSE: *Thanks so much. I really appreciate the information. I'll send you my resume tomorrow and hopefully speak with you soon.*

By just picking up the telephone and using this type of direct approach, you should be able to get four critical things for improving your employability with this type of nonprofit organization:

1. Accurate information about the organization's hiring structure and practices, including whether or not they are currently hiring, and if they compile an in-house resume bank for future reference.

2. Permission to submit your resume and application to a specific person in a position of screening and/or hiring responsibility.

3. Advice and referrals relevant to other organizations in the same occupational field—you tap into the current grapevine of information on who's hiring where for what positions.

4. A relationship established over the telephone with someone who may help you in the future and who hopefully will remember you as that "nice person" they spoke with recently.

Be sure to follow-up this phone call with a nice cover letter and a copy of your resume. These materials should be sent within 24 hours. Wait until two days after the person should have received your letter and then make this follow-up call:

OPENER: *Hi, this is Marcia Taylor. I spoke with you a few days ago about jobs with environmental organizations. I really appreciated your advice. Did you receive the materials you requested I send you last Tuesday?* (Assuming the answer is yes, go on to the next line of questioning.)

CONNECT: *Did you have any questions about my background and interests in environmental issues?* (If the recipient has not read your cover letter and resume carefully, he may look at it now while you are speaking with him over the phone. This question directly connects him to your resume and letter. He's now about to remember you in greater depth by learning more about you as a person and professional.)

REQUEST: *Would you recommend that I contact some other environmental groups?* (It's worth a try to get a referral again. This person may have heard about a vacancy with another group during the past week, since you last asked the question.)

CLOSE: *Again, I want to thank you for looking at my resume and keeping me in your database for future reference. Do let me know if any positions would become available for someone with my qualifications. I'm really interested in promoting the wonderful work of your organization.* (Depending on your situation, you might also inquire about part-time or volunteer positions to literally get your foot in the door.)

This type of follow-up call may accomplish four things related to a possible candidacy:

1. You verify the fact that your materials have indeed been received and imputed into the recipient's system.

2.   You are again remembered as that "nice person" he spoke with before.

3.   The recipient may conduct a preliminary screening interview at this time by asking you a few questions about your background and interests based upon your cover letter and resume. Your answers may result in getting your resume moved into a "should interview sometime" file.

4.   You may get a referral to another environmental organization which has a vacancy or pending vacancy appropriate for your qualifications. This is a great way to develop your networks and plug into the word-of-mouth system that is important to the nonprofit job market.

WRITE DYNAMITE
RESUMES AND LETTERS

Your communication skills tell potential employers a lot about how well you will do in their organizations. Nonprofit organizations are particularly sensitive to communication skills because their livelihoods depend on how well they communicate with their constituencies. They must hire people who have excellent communication skills. Therefore, your resume and letters as well as your telephone conversations and face-to-face interviews are important indicators of your communication skills. Make sure you shine in all of these communication areas.

Some of the most important written communication you will engage in during your job search relates to resumes and letters. Whether sent in the mail or transmitted by fax, your resume and letters should be well focused on your overall goal—get job interviews through direct application or referrals. As you use our organizational listings, or those of others, keep in mind that you will need to write to the contact person you verified in your telephone call. Be sure you always send a resume and/or letter to a specific name. And since individuals move a lot from position to position, and from organization to organization, you must verify the name by telephone **before** you send or transmit information.

On pages 74-85 we include sample resumes and letters based upon principles of effective communication. You should write similar resumes and letters during various stages of your nonprofit job search.

Whenever you send a letter or resume, make sure you follow-up with a phone call. If you have an active application for a specific position, this follow-up call should be aimed at getting a decision in your favor. You want to be remembered, and you want action:

REQUEST: *When would you expect to make a decision?*

Would it be okay if I called you next Friday if I've not heard from you in the meantime?

This line of questioning not only may give you useful information on the decision-making process, it potentially makes you more visible in the eyes of the employer. The individual will remember you as someone he needs to respond to in a timely and specific manner. He'll probably look over your application again—just to be sure he hasn't missed anything.

Chronological Resume

SARAH TAYLOR
2720 Euclid Drive
Philadelphia, Pennsylvania 19110   215/721-1982

OBJECTIVE: A research and public relations position with an association,
where strong communication, research, and analytical skills will
be used for furthering the goals of the association.

EXPERIENCE: Planning Analyst, City of Philadelphia, Pennsylvania.
Developed community-wide plans for public housing and
conducted research in response to requests for zoning vari-
ances. Regularly met with community groups to identify
housing needs, communicate city's policies, and advise on
policies and procedures. Wrote policy papers and reports on
city planning issues. Worked closely with citizen groups,
landlords, contractors, and lawyers representing interests of
various local groups. Developed a new information system
for responding quickly to requests for planning information.
1987-present

Research Associate, Coalition for Community Service
Agencies, Philadelphia, Pennsylvania.
Conducted research, analyzed data, wrote reports, and
lobbied government agencies at both the local and state
levels on various aspects of community service organizations. Research involved interviewing government officials
and representatives of community service groups. Several
reports were responsible for providing greater public assistance to strengthen community service organizations at the
local level. Reports cited by supervisor as "outstanding
contributions to making community service organizations a
central issue on the local government agenda". 1984-1987

EDUCATION: M.A., Public Administration, Temple University, Philadelphia,
Pennsylvania, 1990.

B.A., Political Science, State University of New York,
Plattsburg, New York 1987.

REFERENCES: Available upon request.

Combination Resume

SARAH TAYLOR
2720 Euclid Drive
Philadelphia, Pennsylvania 19110   215/721-1982

OBJECTIVE   A research and public relations position with an association, where strong communication, research, and analytical skills will be used for furthering the goals of the association.

AREAS OF EFFECTIVENESS

RESEARCH   Conducted 22 research projects on various aspects of planning and community service groups. Developed research design, conducted field interviews, and analyzed data. Research resulted in several reports which were responsible for changing local government policies. Consistently cited by supervisors as making "outstanding" contributions to both understanding and action.

PUBLIC RELATIONS   Developed press releases, issued reports, and met regularly with community groups, government officials, contractors, and the press. Devised an innovative information system to respond quickly to requests for information.

COMMUN-ICATION   Authored numerous position papers and major reports on public policy issues for government agencies and community groups. Frequent speaker before community organizations. Conducted several briefings for supervisors, city council members, and the press.

WORK HISTORY   Planning Analyst, City of Philadelphia, Pennsylvania, 1989-95.

Research Associate, Coalition for Community Service Agencies, Philadelphia, Pennsylvania, 1986-1989.

EDUCATION   M.A., Public Administration, Temple University, Philadelphia, Pennsylvania, 1990.

B.A., Political Science, State University of New York, Plattsburg, New York 1987.

PERSONAL   Enjoy developing innovative approaches to public issues which involve research, writing, and frequent contact with government officials and community groups.

Combination Resume—continued

SUPPLEMENTAL INFORMATION   **SARAH TAYLOR**

CONTINUING EDUCATION AND TRAINING

- Completed 15 graduate level hours of research and communication courses directly related to the public service.

- Recently attended several workshops on strengthening research, communication, and community relations skills:

  "Survey Research Methods in Local Government," International City Manager Association, June 4-6, 1995

  "Briefing Techniques," American Management Associations, May 8, 1993

  "Public Speaking," Greater Philadelphia Chamber of Commerce, February 20-21, 1992

  "Effective Report Writing for Public Employees," November 12-13, 1991

  "Planning as a Community Process," American Planning Association, March 21-25, 1989

MAJOR RESEARCH CONDUCTED AND REPORTS AUTHORED

"Making Community Service Organizations Work More Effectively," Coalition for Community Service Agencies, 1994.

"Serving the Community: A Practical Manual for Working With Government and Other Community Organizations," Coalition for Community Service Agencies, 1992.

"Planning Our Housing Future: A Comprehensive Approach to Balanced Growth," City of Philadelphia, 1990.

"City Planning Research: A Manual for Conducting Survey Research in the City of Philadelphia," City of Philadelphia, 1989.

PROFESSIONAL AFFILIATIONS

American Society for Public Administration
American Society of Association Executives
Toastmasters International

EDUCATIONAL HIGHLIGHTS

Working toward Ph.D. in Public Policy with concentration on policy formation and community management.

Earned 4.0/4.0 grade point average in graduate studies.

Functional Resume

SARAH TAYLOR
2720 Euclid Drive
Philadelphia, Pennsylvania 19110   215/721-1982

OBJECTIVE: A research and public relations position with an association, where strong communication, research, and analytical skills will be used for furthering the goals of the association.

EDUCATION: M.A., Public Administration, Temple University, Philadelphia, Pennsylvania, 1990.

B.A., Political Science, State University of New York, Plattsburg, New York, 1987.

MAJOR STRENGTHS: Research

Conducted 22 research projects on various aspects of planning and community service groups. Developed research design, conducted field interviews, and analyzed data. Research resulted in several reports which were responsible for changing local government policies. Consistently cited by supervisors as making "outstanding" contributions to both understanding and action.

Public Relations

Developed press releases, issued reports, and met regularly with community groups, government officials, contractors, and the press. Devised an innovative information system to respond quickly to requests for information.

Communication

Authored numerous position papers and major reports on public policy issues for government agencies and community groups. Frequent speaker before community organizations. Conducted several briefings for supervisors, city council members, and the press.

PERSONAL: Enjoy developing innovative approaches to public issues which involve research, writing, and frequent contact with government officials and community groups.

Resume Letter

2720 Euclid Drive
Philadelphia, PA 19110
April 17, _____

James Weston, Assistant Director
American Association of
    Community Service Organizations
7210 Connecticut Avenue, Suite 223
Washington, DC 20036

Dear Mr. Weston:

AACSO is one of the most important groups providing assistance to community organizations. I know, because I have worked with these groups for several years at both the local and state levels.

My work has been very exciting, but I would now like to contribute to the work of the national association. My experience includes:

Research: Conducted 22 research projects on local planning and community service groups. Research resulted in several reports which significantly altered local government policies.

Public relations: Developed press releases, issued reports, and met regularly with community groups, government officials, contractors, and the press. Devised an innovative information system to respond to quickly requests for information.

Communication: Authored numerous position papers and major reports on public policy issues for agencies and community groups. Frequent speaker before community organizations. Conducted several briefings for supervisors, city council members, and the press.

In addition, I am completing my Ph.D. in Public Policy with emphasis on policy formation and community management.

I would like to meet with you to discuss how my experience and skills relate to the work of AACSO. Since I will be in Washington, DC next month, I would appreciate an opportunity to meet with you at that time. I will call your office on Thursday morning, April 24, to see if we might be able to arrange a mutually convenient time to meet. I especially want to share with you some of the innovative research and public relations work I have done with community service organizations.

I look forward to meeting with you.

Sincerely,

Sarah Taylor

Cover Letter

2720 Euclid Drive
Philadelphia, PA 19110
April 15, _____

James Weston, Assistant Director
American Association of
   Community Service Organizations
7210 Connecticut Avenue, Suite 223
Washington, DC 20036

Dear Mr. Weston:

I enclose my resume in response to your announcement in The Washington Post for a Community Research Analyst.

I am especially interested in this position for several reasons. First, I have six years of thoroughly enjoyable experience in working closely with community service organizations at the local and state levels. Second, I have conducted several practical studies of community service organizations which have resulted in strengthening their roles at the local level. Finally, my research work has placed me at the center of the policy process where I have worked effectively with government officials and other community groups.

I would appreciate an opportunity to meet with you to discuss how my experience might best relate to your needs. My combined research and community relations approach may be of special interest to you since it has resulted in some innovative approaches to community action. I will call your office on Tuesday morning April 22, to see if your schedule would permit such a meeting.

I look forward to learning more about your research needs and sharing some of my experiences with you.

Sincerely,

Sarah Taylor

Approach Letter: Referral

2720 Euclid Drive
Philadelphia, PA 19110
April 8, ____

James Weston, Assistant Director
American Association of
    Community Service Organizations
7210 Connecticut Avenue, Suite 223
Washington, DC 20036

Dear Mr. Weston:

Alice White suggested that I contact you about my interest in community service organizations. She enthusiastically mentioned you as one of the best people to talk to about careers in this public service field.

I am leaving local government after three years of progressively responsible experience in community planning where I worked extensively with community service organizations. But before I decide to seek a career in this field as well as relocate, I believe I would benefit greatly from your experience and insights into this field. Your advice would be very helpful at this stage in my career.

I will be in Washington during the seek of April 21-25. Would it be possible for us to meet briefly to discuss my career plans? I have several concerns you might be most helpful in clarifying. I will call your office on Thursday morning, April 15, to see if your schedule would permit such a meeting.

Sincerely,

Sarah Taylor

Approach Letter: Cold Turkey

2720 Euclid Drive
Philadelphia, PA 19110
March 23, _____

James Weston, Assistant Director
American Association of
    Community Service Organizations
7210 Connecticut Avenue, Suite 223
Washington, DC 20036

Dear Mr. Weston:

I have been most impressed by your work with community service organizations in Philadelphia. Indeed, the recent article appearing in Association Trends on your promotion to assistant director of AACSO stressed what I learned a long time ago here in Philadelphia—you have an exceptional talent to get the local organization to work together in pursuing the national agenda of AACSO. Congratulations on a well deserved promotion!

Your public service career with community service organizations is one I hope to emulate. After six enjoyable years of working with these organizations at the local and state levels, I am convinced I want to pursue a long-term career in this field and especially from a much broader national perspective. My research and public relations work with these groups may also be of interest to you.

Would it be possible for us to meet briefly to discuss my career interests in this field? I believe your advice would be most valuable in helping me better define my future with community service organizations.

I will be in Washington, DC during the week of April 21-25. Perhaps your schedule would permit a meeting during that week. I will call your office on Tuesday morning, April 8, to see if such a meeting would be possible.

I look forward to meeting you and learning from your experience.

Sincerely,

Sarah Taylor

Thank-You Letter:
Post-Informational Interview

2720 Euclid Drive
Philadelphia, PA 19110
March 23, _____

James Weston, Assistant Director
American Association of
    Community Service Organizations
7210 Connecticut Avenue, Suite 223
Washington, DC 20036

Dear Mr. Weston:

Our meeting yesterday was truly informative and extremely useful in helping me clarify various concerns regarding careers with community service organizations. Your experience and knowledge of this field is most impressive.

I want to thank you again for taking the time from your busy schedule to meet with me. Your suggestions for strengthening my resume were very helpful. I am now revising the resume in light of your thoughtful advice. I will sent you a copy of the revised resume next week.

Following your advice, I will contact Marilyn Plante tomorrow to see if she might have or know of any opportunities for someone with my interests and qualifications. I will give her your regards.

I hope to have a chance to meet with you again sometime.

Sincerely,

Sarah Taylor

Thank-You Letter:
Post-Job Interview

2720 Euclid Drive
Philadelphia, PA 19110
March 23, _____

James Weston, Assistant Director
American Association of
   Community Service Organizations
7210 Connecticut Avenue, Suite 223
Washington, DC 20036

Dear Mr. Weston:

I want to thank you again for the opportunity to interview for the Community Research Analyst position. You and your staff were most helpful in clarifying many questions about this position and AACSO.

Our meeting further convinced me that this position is ideally suited for my interests, skills, and experience. My prior research and public relations work with community service agencies at the local and state levels has prepared me well for this position. I am committed to giving AACSO my very best effort.

I look forward to meeting with you again to further discuss my candidacy.

Sincerely,

Sarah Taylor

Thank-You Letter:
Job Rejection

2720 Euclid Drive
Philadelphia, PA 19110
March 23, _____

James Weston, Assistant Director
American Association of
    Community Service Organizations
7210 Connecticut Avenue, Suite 223
Washington, DC 20036

Dear Mr. Weston:

I want to thank you again for considering me for the Community Research Analyst position. Although I am disappointed with the outcome, I appreciated the opportunity and learned a great deal about AACSO. I am especially pleased with the highly professional manner in which you and your staff conducted the interview.

Please keep me in mind for future vacancies. I have a strong interest in AACSO which will certainly continue in the future. I believe I could contribute a great deal to AACSO. I am sure I would work well with you and your staff.

Best wishes.

Sincerely,

Sarah Taylor

Thank-You Letter:
Job Offer Acceptance

2720 Euclid Drive
Philadelphia, PA 19110
March 23, ____

James Weston, Assistant Director
American Association of
    Community Service Organizations
7210 Connecticut Avenue, Suite 223
Washington, DC 20036

Dear Mr. Weston:

I am pleased to accept your offer and look forward to joining AACSO later this month.

The Community Research Analyst position is ideally suited to my interests, skills, and experience. I will give you and AACSO my very best effort.

I understand I will begin work on May 14. Please contact me if I need to complete any paperwork prior to this starting date.

Thank you again for your consideration and confidence.

Sincerely,

Sarah Taylor

7

THE START-UP DIRECTORY TO NONPROFIT ORGANIZATIONS

*T*he nonprofit organizations profiled in this chapter represent some of the most popular types of organizations associated with the nonprofit world. Each listing includes the organization's purpose, activities, budget, and number of employees. We include the organization's name, address, and phone number. If you decide to contact an organization, do what we advised in Chapter 6—call the organization to verify its current address and to get the name of the individual who handles personnel matters. In the case of very small nonprofits, this individual may be the director of the organization. With larger organizations, this person may be a personnel manager or the director of the human resources department. In any case, be sure you get a specific name to whom you will direct your communication.

ARTS AND ENTERTAINMENT

The nonprofit organizations profiled in this section represent a wide variety of interests related to the arts and entertainment—children, women, minorities, producers, artists, free speech, communication, and legal issues. While most of these organizations are small—operating on budgets in the $150,000 to $350,000 range and using a large number of volunteers and interns—these organizations do offer many full-time and part-time positions. Various positions include director, program assistants, program coordinators, grantwriters, publicists, writers, editors, grassroots fundraisers, foundation fundraisers, issue experts, lobbyists, administrative assistants, attorneys, office managers, bookkeepers, accountants, stage managers, and receptionists. Entry-level positions tend to pay $14,000 to $20,000 a year. Other positions may pay in the $25,000 to $35,000 range. These nonprofit organizations are especially in need of two types of fundraisers—grassroots and foundation. Being small organizations, much of the work will be multi-faceted and entail a great deal of responsibility.

ARTISTS UNLIMITED
158 Thomas Street, Suite 14
Seattle, WA 98109
Tel. 206/441-8480

Purpose: To provide education on professional development in the arts to adults with disabilities.
Activity: Research, training, technical assistance, direct service.
Budget: $150,000
Employees: Part-time: 7; Volunteers: 75; Interns: varies

CALIFORNIA LAWYERS FOR THE ARTS
Fort Mason Center
Building C, Room 255
San Francisco, CA 94123
Tel. 415/775-7200

Purpose: To provide legal services, education, and self-help information to artists, performers, and arts organizations of all disciplines. Programs and services are designed to respond to the needs of the California arts community and help artists understand and apply legal concepts for their benefit. A collaborative mediation project provides alternative dispute resolution services throughout the country.

Activity: Legal services, education, research, training.
Budget: $440,000
Employees: Full-time: 9; Part-time: 3; Volunteers: 15; Interns: 5

CENTER FOR SAFETY
IN THE ARTS
5 Beekman Street, Suite 820
New York, NY 10038
Tel. 212/227-6220

Purpose: To provide education and information on health and safety hazards and precautions in the visual and performing arts.
Activity: Research, lobbying, publications, public education, training and technical assistance, answering written and telephone inquiries on specific problems.
Budget: $250,000
Employees: Full-time: 11; Part-time: varies; Volunteers: 1; Interns: 1

CHILDREN'S ART FOUNDATION
765 Cedar Street, Suite 201
Santa Cruz, CA 95060
Tel. 408/426-5557

Purpose: To encourage childrens' creativity through educational and publication programs.
Activity: Art school and publications.
Budget: $350,000
Employees: Full-time: 3; Part-time: 6; Volunteers: 4; Interns: none

EMPOWERMENT PROJECT
3403 Highway 54 West
Chapel Hill, NC 27516
Tel. 919/967-1963

Purpose: To provide facilities, training and other support for independent producers, artists, activists and organizations to work toward democratizing access to the media and to provide the resources necessary to put the power of media in the hands of individuals and organizations working to further important human purposes.
Activity: Community organizing, training and technical assistance, direct action, research.
Budget: $355,000
Employees: Full-time: 4; Part-time: 1; Volunteers: 30; Interns: 9

FILM NEWS NOW FOUNDATION
100 Bleecker Street
Suite 12D
New York, NY 10012
Tel. 212/998-1577

Purpose: To advance the presence and involvement of people of color and women in the media field by assisting, encouraging, and providing services and consultations to minority as well as women producers.
Activity: Research, publications, public education, training and technical assistance, lobbying, and community organizing.
Budget: $900,000
Employees: Full-time: 3; Part-time: 2; Volunteers: 2; Interns: 2

LIBRARY THEATRE, INC.
6925 Willow Street, NW
Washington, DC 20012
Tel. 202/291-4800

Purpose: To produce theater and media programs to educate and entertain children and their families. Uses programming to enrich children culturally as well as to address social and educational issues.
Activity: Public education through programs on peer pressure, drug abuse, the importance of hard work, and overcoming disabilities and gender stereotypes, and publications.
Budget: $350,000
Employees: Full-time: 6; Part-time: varies; Volunteers: 20+; Interns: varies

LIVING STAGE THEATRE COMPANY
6th and Main Avenue, SW
Washington, DC 20024
Tel. 202/554-9066

Purpose: To use improvisational theater techniques in a performance/workshop format working with groups of youth and adults in the inner city, helping them to rediscover their creativity, thereby promoting more positive life choices.
Activity: Human services, training, technical assistance.
Budget: $650,000
Employees: 17; Part-time: 1; Volunteers: 3; Interns: 3

MINNEAPOLIS TELECOMMUNICATIONS NETWORK
125 SE Main Street
Minneapolis, MN 55414
Tel. 612/331-8575

Purpose: To train people to use and create programs which promote free speech, communication within cultures, educate the general public about neighborhoods and other cultures.
Activity: Provide training and technical assistance, promote community organizing and public education.
Budget: $650,000
Employees: Full-time: 15; Part-time: 7; Volunteers: 500; Interns: 5

NATIONAL CAMPAIGN FOR FREEDOM OF EXPRESSION
1402 3rd Avenue, #421
Seattle, WA 98101
Tel. 206/340-9301

Purpose: To fight censorship and to protect and extend the First Amendment right to freedom of artistic expression.
Activity: Research, lobbying, litigation, publications, community organizing, public education, media education/advocacy.
Budget: $250,000
Employees: Full-time: 3; Part-time: 3; Volunteers: varies; Interns: 1

VOLUNTEER LAWYERS FOR THE ARTS
1 East 53rd Street
6th Floor
New York, NY 10022
Tel. 212/319-2787

Purpose: To provide arts-related legal assistance to artists and arts organizations in all creative fields who cannot afford private counsel. VLA also works to prevent legal entanglements through education programs, including seminars, publications, and the maintenance of an Art Law Library.
Activity: Legal services to indigent artists and emerging or small arts organizations. Research, publications, public education and lobbying.
Budget: $500,000
Employees: Full-time: 7; Part-time: 3; Volunteers: 5, plus 800 lawyers; Interns: 35

WOMEN MAKE MOVIES
462 Broadway, Suite 500
New York, NY 10013
Tel. 212/925-0606

Purpose: To facilitate production, promotion and distribution of women's films and videotapes. Also provide support services to emerging and established women film and video artists.
Activity: Training and technical assistance, publications, community organizing, and lobbying.
Budget: $1,125,000
Employees: Full-time: 9; Part-time: 2; Volunteers: 4; Interns: 4

CIVIL LIBERTIES AND CIVIL RIGHTS

Who defends civil liberties and fights for civil rights? Some might say lawyers or the down-trodden themselves. The truth is that many nonprofit groups are organized to deal with these issues. The nonprofit organizations appearing in this section represent a wide variety of interests and groups related to civil liberties and civil rights—freedom, immigration, AIDS, law, handicapped, human rights, minorities, and women. Many of these groups, such as the AIDS Project of Los Angeles and Americans for Democratic Action, also should appear in the sections on medical/health care and political/government reform.

Most of the organizations in this section also are relatively small, with budgets under $2 million and with fewer than 25 employees. However, a few of these organizations are medium in size, with budgets over $20 million and staffs in excess of 200.

Many of our civil liberties and civil rights organizations have been at the forefront in fighting for change. Some have made significant contributions to the nation's civil rights movement. Individuals working for these organizations tend to be passionately committed to change. Most of these nonprofits are relatively liberal groups seeking to make significant changes in government policies.

AFRICA FUND
198 Broadway, Room 402
New York, NY 10038
Tel. 212/962-1210

Purpose: To support the struggle for African freedom and independence through assistance and educational campaigns in the U.S.
Activity: Research, public education, and publications.
Budget: $600,000
Employees: Full-time: 7; Part-time: 3; Volunteers: varies; Interns: varies

AIDS PROJECT—LOS ANGELES
1313 N. Vine Street
Los Angeles, CA 90028
Tel. 213/993-1600

Purpose: To be a direct provider of, and resource for, HIV/AIDS services and information, and an advocate at all levels of government for people with HIV/AIDS.

Activity: Lobbying, publications, human services community organizing, public education, training and technical assistance.
Budget: $19,000,000
Employees: Full-time: 220; Part-time: 20; Volunteers: 2,500; Interns: varies

AMERICAN BAR ASSOCIATION, PUBLIC SERVICES DIVISION
1800 M Street, NW
Washington, DC 20036
Tel. 202/331-2276

Purpose: To provide leadership in identification, development and reform of law and law-related policies that promote the ideals of a just society and ensure equal rights and protections for all, particularly vulnerable populations.
Activity: Research, publications and videos, public education, training and technical assistance nationwide, symposia, workshops and conferences, model legislation, policy development for American Bar Association, speeches and professional papers.
Budget: $2,000,000
Employees: Full-time: 30; Part-time: 5; Volunteers: 5; Interns: varies

AMERICAN CIVIL LIBERTIES UNION (ACLU)
Washington Office
122 Maryland Avenue, NE
Washington, DC 20002
Tel. 202/544-1681

Purpose: To secure the enactment of legislation which expands the rights and liberties of Americans and to prevent the enactment of legislation that interferes with such rights.
Activity: Lobbying, research, and publications.
Budget: $1,000,000
Employees: Full-time: 19; Part-time: None; Volunteers: 3; Interns: 10-15

AMERICAN CIVIL LIBERTIES UNION OF SOUTHERN CALIFORNIA
1616 Beverly Blvd.
Los Angeles, CA 90026
Tel. 213/977-9500

Purpose: To assure that the Bill of Rights and amendments to the Constitution that guard against unwarranted governmental control, are preserved.

Activity: Litigation, lobbying, community organizing, public education, research, and publications.
Budget: $2,500,000
Employees: Full-time: 31; Part-time: None; Volunteers: 5; Interns: 20 law students (summer)

AMERICAN COUNCIL OF THE BLIND
1155 15th Street NW, Suite 720
Washington,. DC 20005
Tel. 202/467-5081

Purpose: To promote the independence, dignity and well-being of blind, and visually impaired people.
Activity: Lobbying, litigation, publications, direct action, public education, community organizing, and human services.
Budget: $1,000,000
Employees: Full-time: 12; Part-time: None; Volunteers: None; Interns: varies

AMERICAN FOUNDATION FOR THE BLIND
15 West 16th Street
New York, NY 10011
Tel. 212/620-2000
(Regional centers in Chicago, Dallas, San Francisco
and Washington, DC)

Purpose: To enable persons who are blind or visually impaired to achieve equality of access and opportunity that will ensure freedom of choice in their lives.
Activity: Research, lobbying, publications, public education, training and technical assistance.
Budget: $12,000,000
Employees: Full-time: 125; Part-time: varies; Volunteers: varies; Interns: varies

AMERICANS FOR DEMOCRATIC ACTION
1625 K Street NW, Suite 210
Washington, DC 20006
Tel. 202/785-5980
(Other offices in Winston-Salem, NC; Tempe, AZ; and Chicago)

Purpose: To educate the American public as to the significant issues; to lobby on behalf of these issues; to work through their public action committee (PAC) in supporting candidates whose views are similar to

ADA's; to produce publications and analysis for mass distribution.
Activity: Lobbying, publications, community organizing, public education, and direct action.
Budget: $500,000
Employees: Full-time 9; Part-time: 3; Volunteers: varies; Interns: 5

CENTER FOR IMMIGRANTS RIGHTS
48 Saint Marks Place, 4th Floor
New York, NY 10003
Tel. 212/505-6890

Purpose: To provide legal assistance, community outreach and education, policy advocacy and technical support in defending the rights of immigrant newcomers, documented and undocumented, in the areas of immigration, employment rights, access to public entitlements/health and civil rights.
Activity: Public education, training and technical assistance, community organizing, publications, litigation, lobbying and research.
Budget: $330,000
Employees: Full-time: 6; Part-time: 2; Volunteers: 5, Interns: 5

CENTER ON BUDGET AND POLICY PRIORITIES
777 N. Capitol Street NE, Suite 705
Washington, DC 20002
Tel. 202/408-1080

Purpose: To provide research and analysis which focuses on the impact of changes in Federal and state policies on low-income Americans.
Activity: Publications, training and technical assistance, research, public education, and lobbying.
Budget: $2,900,000
Employees: Full-time: 36; Part-time: 7; Volunteers: none; Interns 5

CITIZENS ACTION COALITION OF INDIANA
3951 N. Meridian St. #300
Indianapolis, IN 46208
Tel. 317/921-1120

Purpose: To advocate public interest in energy, utility, health care, and environmental policies and issues concerning small farmers.
Activity: Research, lobbying, community organizing, public education, litigation, and publications.
Budget: $2,500,000

Employees: Full-time: 85; Part-time: 30; Volunteers: 30; Interns: none, but will accept applications

COMMITTEE TO PROTECT JOURNALISTS
330 7th Avenue, 12th Floor
New York, NY 10001
Tel. 212/465-1004

Purpose: To promote press freedoms around the world.
Activity: Publications, research and direct action, consisting of monitoring events around the world, confirming facts, protesting where appropriate, sharing information with other professional groups, publicizing cases and publishing reports and periodicals.
Budget: $430,000
Employees: Full-time: 11; Part-time: 1; Volunteers: varies; Interns: varies

DISABILITY RIGHTS EDUCATION AND DEFENSE FUND
2212 6th Street
Berkeley, CA 94710
Tel. 510/644-2555
(Other office in Washington, DC)

Purpose: To provide legal advice and representation for people with disabilities and parents of children with disabilities, especially civil rights in regards to school, employment, housing, and educating local, state and national representatives regarding disability.
Activity: Training and technical assistance, national policy monitoring, litigation, and community organizing.
Budget: $500,000
Employees: Full-time: 19; Part-time: None; Volunteers: varies; Interns: 5-10

EQUAL RIGHTS ADVOCATES
1663 Mission Street
Suite 550
San Francisco, CA 94103
Tel. 510/621-0672

Purpose: To address sex and race-based discrimination including legal representation, public education, advice and counseling, coalition building, media relations and public policy advocacy.
Activity: Litigation, public education, advice and counseling, publications, community organizing, training and technical assistance, public policy advocacy, and grassroots lobbying.

Budget: $1,000,000
Employees: Full-time: 12; Part-time: 3; Volunteers: varies; Interns: varies

FRIENDS COMMITTEE ON NATIONAL LEGISLATION
245 Second Street NE
Washington, DC 20002
Tel. 202/547-6000

Purpose: To bring Quaker values to bear on public policy. FCNL's goals are world peace, equity and justice for all, civil rights, environmental quality, and economic justice.
Activity: Lobbying, research and education, and publications.
Budget: $1,000,000
Employees: Full-time: 22; Part-time: varies, Volunteers: many; Interns: 4

HUMAN RIGHTS CAMPAIGN FUND
1012 14th Street NW
Suite 607
Washington, DC 20005
Tel. 202/628-4160
(Other offices in Atlanta and Chicago)

Purpose: To secure full civil rights for lesbians and gay men and responsible policies on AIDS.
Activity: Research, lobbying, publications, community organizing and public education.
Budget: $3,500,000
Employees: Full-time: 26; Part-time: none; Volunteers: 10; Interns: 5

INDIAN LAW RESOURCE CENTER
601 E Street SE
Washington, DC 20003
Tel. 202/547-2800

Purpose: To provide legal help without charge to Indian nations and tribes in major cases of important Indian rights.
Activity: Research, litigation, training and technical assistance, publications, and public education.
Budget: $400,000
Employees: Full-time: 8; Part-time: 0; Volunteers: 0; Interns: 1

LAWYERS' COMMITTEE FOR CIVIL RIGHTS UNDER THE LAW
1450 G Street NW, Suite 400
Washington, DC 20005
Tel. 202/662-8600

Purpose: To provide quality legal services for poor and minorities on major civil and Constitutional rights cases. Represents clients in suits alleging unlawful racial discrimination and influence the development and application of civil rights law.
Activity: Research, litigation in cases involving voting rights, discrimination, education, housing, and minority business enterprise.
Budget: $4,500,000
Employees: Full-time: 28; Part-time: 2; Volunteers: none; Interns: 8

MEXICAN AMERICAN LEGAL DEFENSE AND EDUCATIONAL FUND
634 South Spring Street, 11th Floor
Los Angeles, CA 90014
Tel. 213/629-2512
(Other offices in San Francisco; Washington, DC; San Antonio; Chicago; Sacramento; Fresno; Santa Ana; and Detroit)

Purpose: To promote and protect the civil rights of U.S. Latinos through class action litigation, advocacy and community education.
Activity: Lobbying, litigation, publications, direct action, public education, leadership and development.
Budget: $4,300,000
Employees: Full-time: 60; Part-time: none; Volunteers: varies; Interns: varies

NAACP LEGAL DEFENSE AND EDUCATIONAL FUND—LOS ANGELES
315 W. 9th Street, Suite 208
Los Angeles, CA 90025
Tel. 213/624-2405
(Other office in New York City)

Purpose: To undertake civil rights litigation and advocacy in a variety of discrimination areas including: education, housing, voting rights, employment, health, environmental justice, poverty, and criminal justice.
Activity: Litigation, training and technical assistance.
Budget: $9,500,000
Employees: Full-time: 9; Part-time: none; Volunteers: 1; Interns: 5

NAACP LEGAL DEFENSE AND
EDUCATIONAL FUND, INC.
99 Hudson Street, 16th Floor
New York, NY 10013
Tel. 212/219-1900
(Other offices in Los Angeles and Washington, DC)

Purpose: To bring civil rights litigation on behalf of African Americans in areas of employment, housing, voting, education, health care, poverty and justice and capital punishment.
Activity: Litigation, research, lobbying, community organizing, and scholarships.
Budget: $9,000,000
Employees: Full-time: 75; Part-time: 3; Volunteers: none; Interns: 3

NATIONAL CAUCUS AND CENTER
ON BLACK AGED, INC.
1424 K Street NW, Suite 500
Washington, DC 20005
Tel. 202/637-8400
(Other offices in Atlanta, Chicago, Baltimore,
Cleveland, Philadelphia, Raleigh, NC, and Stuttgart, AZ)

Purpose: To improve the quality of life for African American elderly—especially those who are low income.
Activity: Lobbying, publications, human services, direct action, public education, training and technical assistance.
Budget: $1,700,000
Employees: Full-time: 26; Part-time: 2; Volunteers: none; Interns: 7

NATIONAL URBAN LEAGUE, INC.
500 East 62nd Street
New York, NY 10021
Tel. 212/310-9000

Purpose: To assist African Americans in the achievement of social and economic equality in such crucial areas as educational attainment, employment and economic self-sufficiency.
Activity: Advocacy, research, human services, community organizing, publications, public education, training and technical assistance.
Budget: $27,000,000
Employees: Full-time: 200; Part-time: varies; Volunteers: 30,000 plus; Interns: varies

PEOPLE FOR THE AMERICAN WAY
2000 M Street NW
Suite 400
Washington, DC 20036
Tel. 202/467-4999
(Other offices in Los Angeles and New York City)

Purpose: To promote and protect individual liberties including First Amendment rights and the right to privacy.
Activity: Research, lobbying, litigation, publications, community organizing, and public education.
Budget: $7,600,000
Employees: Full-time: 49; Part-time: 3; Volunteers: 25; Interns: 10

PUERTO RICAN LEGAL DEFENSE AND EDUCATION FUND
99 Hudson Street
14th Floor
New York, NY 10013
Tel. 212/219-3360

Purpose: To protect the civil rights of Puerto Ricans and other Latinos and to ensure their equal protection under the law.
Activity: Litigation, legal education training, community education, and advocacy.
Budget: $1,400,000
Employees: Full-time: 19; Part-time: none; Volunteers: varies; Interns: varies

THE URBAN INSTITUTE
2100 M Street NW
Washington, DC 20037
Tel. 202/833-7200

Purpose: To conduct research, evaluations, and policy analysis related to social and economic issues facing the U.S. (or related to the same issues in developing nations); to improve government decisions and their implementation; and to facilitate informed debate and decision-making by policy makers.
Activity: Research, publications, training and technical assistance.
Budget: $21,000,000
Employees: Full-time: 220; Part-time: 10; Volunteers: varies; Interns: 10

WOMEN'S LEGAL DEFENSE FUND
1875 Connecticut Ave. NW, Suite 710
Washington, DC 20009
Tel. 202/986-2600

Purpose: To help women become full and equal participants in their public and private lives; WLDF advocates public policies that focus on work and family concerns.
Activity: Lobbying, litigation, publications, community organizing, public education, training and technical assistance.
Budget: $1,800,000
Employees: Full-time; 24; Part-time: varies; Volunteers: varies; Interns: varies

WORLD INSTITUTE ON DISABILITY
510 16th Street
Oakland, CA 94612
Tel. 415/763-4100

Purpose: To use research, public education, training and model program development as a means to create a more accessible and supportive society for all people—disabled and nondisabled alike.
Activity: Public education, research, training and technical assistance, publications, direct action, and community organizing.
Budget: $2,500,000
Employees: Full-time: 30; Part-time: 3; Volunteers: 5; Interns: 4

CONSUMER ADVOCACY

The organizations presented in this section fit the stereotypical nonprofit organization profile—advocate a particular consumer issue and employ individuals who are passionately committed to consumer issues. Here you will find everything from the Center for Auto Safety to the Older Persons Action Group. These groups do a great deal of research and lobbying. They sponsor some of the most important legislation affecting consumers. Many of these groups have been at the forefront in getting government to change laws concerning housing, health care, insurance reform, public education, food labeling, utility rates, business practices, and environmental control. Most of these nonprofits are relatively small organizations with budgets under $2 million and staffs under 20. However, you'll find exceptions to this rule as in the case of the Consumers Union which operates with a $76 million annual budget and with a staff of 348 full-time employees.

AMERICAN COUNCIL OF THE BLIND
1155 15th Street NW
Suite 720
Washington, DC 20005
Tel. 202/467-5081

Purpose: To promote the independence, dignity and well-being of blind and visually impaired people.
Activity: Lobbying, litigation, publications, direct action, public education and community organizing, and human services.
Budget: $1,000,000
Employees: Full-time: 12; Part-time: none; Interns: varies

CALIFORNIA PUBLIC INTEREST RESEARCH GROUP
1147 South Robertson Blvd.
Suite 203
Los Angeles, CA 90035
Tel. 213/278-9244

Purpose: To conduct research and advocacy on environmental and consumer issues in California.
Activity: Research, lobbying, litigation, publications, community organizing, and public education.

Budget: $750,000
Employees: Full-time: 62; Part-time: 15; Volunteers: varies; Interns: varies

CENTER FOR AUTO SAFETY
2001 S Street NW
Suite 410
Washington, DC 20009
Tel. 202/328-7700

Purpose: To conduct research and advocacy regarding fuel efficiency and emissions, vehicle safety, economy and reliability.
Activity: Research, public education, training and technical assistance, publications, and litigation.
Budget: $750,000
Employees: Full-time: 13; Interns: 6

CITIZENS ADVICE BUREAU, INC.
2054 Morris Avenue
Bronx, NY 10453
Tel. 212/365-0910
(Other office in New York City)

Purpose: To assist low-income families and senior citizens to meet survival needs and to support policy efforts aimed at eradication of poverty.
Activity: Human services, training and technical assistance, and community organizing.
Budget: $1,300,000
Employees: Full-time: 200; Volunteers: 6; Interns: 8

CITIZENS UTILITY BOARD
208 South LaSalle
Suite 584
Chicago, IL 60604
Tel. 312/263-4282
(Other office in Springfield, IL)

Purpose: To represent the interests of residential and small business utility ratepayers in matters before regulatory agencies, the Illinois General Assembly and other jurisdictions.
Activity: Litigation, community organizing, public education, lobbying, publications, research, and human services.
Budget: $1,800,000
Employees: Full-time: 11; Part-time: 5; Volunteers: 1; Interns: 3

CO-OP AMERICA
1850 M Street NW
Suite 700
Washington, DC 20036
Tel. 202/872-5307

Purpose: To create a just and sustainable society by working in four program areas: to encourage corporate responsibility; to help socially responsible businesses emerge and thrive; to educate consumers about creating social change; and to create sustainable communities.
Activity: Research, public education, publications, networking and creating an "alternative marketplace."
Budget: $2,500,000
Employees: Full-time: 24; Part-time: 4; Interns: 25

COLORADO PUBLIC INTEREST RESEARCH GROUP
1724 Gilpin Street
Denver, CO 80218
Tel. 303/355-1861
(Other offices in Boulder, Fort Collins,
Greeley, Gunnison, and Pueblo)

Purpose: To conduct research and advocacy on environmental, consumer and democracy issues to further the public interest.
Activity: Lobbying, community organizing, public education, training and technical assistance, research and publications.
Budget: $250,000
Employees: Full-time: 18; Part-time: varies; Volunteers: 10; Interns: 5

CONSUMER FEDERATION OF AMERICA
1424 16th Street NW
Suite 604
Washington, DC 20036
Tel. 202/387-6121

Purpose: To advocate and educate for the advancement of pro-consumer policy on a variety of issues before Congress, regulatory agencies and the courts.
Activity: Advocacy, education, and member services.
Budget: $1,200,000
Employees: Full-time: 14; Part-time: 4; Interns: 3

CONSUMERS UNION
256 Washington Street
Mount Vernon, NY 10553
Tel. 914/378-2000
(Other offices in Washington, DC; San Francisco;
and Austin, TX)

Purpose: To provide consumers with information and advice on goods,
services, health and personal finance and to initiate/cooperate with individual
and group efforts to maintain and enhance the quality of life for consumers.
Activity: Research, lobbying, litigation, publications, community organizing,
direct action, public education, training and technical assistance.
Budget: $76,000,000
Employees: Full-time: 348; Part-time: varies; Volunteers: varies; Interns:
varies

FLORIDA PUBLIC INTEREST RESEARCH GROUP
420 East Call Street
Tallahassee, FL 32301
Tel. 904/224-5304
(Other offices in Tampa and Miami)

Purpose: To research, educate, and advocate on environmental and
consumer protection issues.
Activity: Lobbying and organizing, public education, and research.
Budget: $200,000
Employees: Full-time: 9; Part-time: varies; Volunteers: varies; Interns: varies

HEALTH CARE FOR ALL
30 Winter Street
Suite 1007
Boston, MA 02108
Tel. 617/350-7279

Purpose: To promote reform of the health care system on both state and
national levels.
Activity: Community organizing, public education, human services, research,
publications, lobbying, direct action, and litigation.
Budget: $400,000
Employees: Full-time: 8; Part-time: 2; Volunteers: 10; Interns: 6

HOUSING AND CREDIT COUNSELING, INC.
1195 SW Buchanan, Suite 203
Topeka, KS 66604-1183
Tel. 913/234-0217
(Other offices in Lawrence and Manhattan)

Purpose: To facilitate safe, adequate, affordable and equitable housing situations for all—particularly those of low and moderate income; assist with budgeting and debt repayment alternatives so people can handle their finances on their own and avoid bankruptcy.
Activity: Human services, public education, training and technical assistance, and community organizing.
Budget: $500,000
Employees: Full-time: 21; Part-time: 1; Volunteers: varies; Interns: varies

MASSACHUSETTS PUBLIC INTEREST RESEARCH GROUP
29 Temple Place
Boston, MA 02111
Tel. 617/292-4800

Purpose: To develop policy, coordinate grassroots campaigns, and win legislation to promote environmental preservation, consumer protection, safe energy and corporate and governmental responsibility.
Activity: Lobbying, research, community organizing, fundraising, public education, litigation, and publications.
Budget: $1,200,000
Employees: Full-time: 54; Part-time: 10-20; Volunteers: 5-15; Interns: 10-15

MINNESOTA PUBLIC INTEREST RESEARCH GROUP
2512 Delaware Street SE
Minneapolis, MN 55414
Tel. 612/627-4035
(Other offices in Duluth, Morris, Northfield
and St. Paul)

Purpose: To promote the public interest through research and policy development, legislative advocacy, impact litigation, and grassroots organizing.
Activity: Research, lobbying, litigation, community organizing, and public education.
Budget: $400,000
Employees: Full-time: 15; Part-time: 5-15; Volunteers: 300-500; Interns: 5-25

NATIONAL CONSUMER LAW CENTER
11 Beacon Street
Boston, MA 02108
Tel. 617/523-8010
(Other office in Washington, DC)

Purpose: To provide legal and technical assistance to lawyers representing low-income clients on consumer and energy issues and provide direct representation to low-income clients on these issues in cases of national scope.
Activity: Research, lobbying, litigation, publications, training and technical assistance.
Budget: $2,000,000
Employees: Full-time: 22; Part-time: varies; Volunteers: varies; Interns: varies

NATIONAL CONSUMERS LEAGUE
815 15th Street NW, Suite 928
Washington, DC 20005
Tel. 202/639-8140

Purpose: To represent and provide information to consumers and workers through research, education, and advocacy.
Activity: Public education, direct action, research, publications, community organizing, lobbying and human services.
Budget: $1,000,000
Employees: Full-time: 15; Part-time: 4; Volunteers: 2: Interns: 3

NEW JERSEY CITIZEN ACTION
400 Main Street
Hackensack, NJ 07601
201/488-2804
(Other offices in New Brunswick, Trenton,
Woodbury, and Collingswood)

Purpose: To increase citizen participation in the democratic process on issues such as toxic chemicals, fair banking, affordable housing and health care, insurance reform, and family leave.
Activity: Lobbying, community organizing, direct action, education.
Budget: $600,000
Employees: Full-time: 63; Part-time: 2; Volunteers: 4; Interns: 6

NEW YORK PUBLIC INTEREST RESEARCH GROUP, INC.
9 Murray Street
New York, NY 10007-2272
Tel. 212/349-6460
(Other offices in Buffalo, Syracuse, Cortland, Binghamton,
Albany, New Paltz, Purchase, Oswego, Huntington, Stony
Brook, Garden City, Old Westbury, and Washington, DC)

Purpose: To advocate for a cleaner environment, consumer protection, fair and open government, mass transit, quality health care, better funding for higher education and issues of social justice.
Activity: Research, lobbying, student organizing, litigation, publications, community organizing, public education, training and technical assistance, and legal action.
Budget: $4,000,000
Employees: Full-time: 98; Part-time: varies; Volunteers: varies; Interns 6-12

OFFICE OF THE CONSUMERS' COUNSEL
77 South High Street
15th Floor
Columbus, OH 43266-0550
Tel. 614/466-8574

Purpose: To represent Ohio's residential public utility consumers before state and federal courts, legislative and regulatory bodies. To provide professional, innovative and accountable advocacy.
Activity: Litigation and negotiation, research, lobbying, publications, public education, training and technical assistance.
Budget: $4,800,000
Employees: Full-time: 64; Interns: varies

OHIO CITIZEN ACTION
402 Terminal Tower
50 Public Square
Cleveland, OH 44113
Tel. 216/861-5200
(Other offices in Akron, Cincinnati, Toledo,
Columbus, and Dayton)

Purpose: To promote and assist citizen action as the basis for democratic change.
Activity: Research, lobbying, publications, community organizing, direct action, public education, training and technical assistance, elections, and litigation.

Budget: $4,000,000
Employees: Full-time: 172; Part-time: varies; Volunteers: varies; Interns: varies

OLDER PERSONS ACTION GROUP, INC.
325 E. Third Avenue
Suite 300
Anchorage, AK 99501
Tel. 907/276-1059
(Other office in Wasilla, AK)

Purpose: To improve services, develop programs, educate, promote and implement changes to foster self-determination of older Alaskan citizens.
Activity: Training and technical assistance, publications, research, direct action, and public education.
Budget: $800,000
Employees: Full-time: 24; Part-time: 21; Volunteers: 15; Interns: will accept applications

OREGON STATE PUBLIC INTEREST RESEARCH GROUP
1536 SE 11th Street
Portland, OR 97214
Tel. 503/231-4181
(Other office in Eugene, OR)

Purpose: To conduct independent research, monitor government and corporate actions, and advocate reforms to benefit the public—primarily in the areas of environmental protection, consumer rights, and government reform.
Activity: Community organizing, research, public education, lobbying, publications, and direct action.
Budget: $500,000
Employees: Full-time: 18; Volunteers: varies; Interns: varies

UNITED STATES PUBLIC INTEREST RESEARCH GROUP
215 Pennsylvania Avenue SE
Washington, DC 20003
Tel. 202/546-9707

Purpose: To advocate for environmental protection, consumer protection, energy and government reform.

Activity: Lobbying, community organizing, public education, research and publications.
Budget: $380,000
Employees: 36; Part-time: 16; Interns: 10

ECONOMIC DEVELOPMENT

Most of the organizations in this section focus on issues relating to poverty, hunger, community development, cooperatives, credit unions, investment, and income generation. These organizations represent a combination of approaches—organizing self-help initiatives to empower individuals and communities to create self-sustaining development and lobbying government for changes in legislation.

While you will find numerous nonprofit organizations involved with economic development issues, most are very small with annual budgets under $1,000,000 and with fewer than 20 full-time employees. These organizations do offer numerous volunteer opportunities.

ACCION INTERNATIONAL
130 Prospect Street
Cambridge, MA 02139
Tel. 617/492-4930
(Other offices in New York, NY: Albuquerque, NM;
San Antonio, TX; and Washington, DC)

Purpose: To fight poverty and hunger by encouraging the economic self-reliance of impoverished working men and women in the Americas.
Activity: Publications and training and technical assistance.
Budget: $4,000,000
Employees: Full-time: 15; Part-time: 1; Volunteers: varies; Interns: varies

CHICANOS POR LA CAUSA, INC.
1112 East Buckeye Road
Phoenix, AZ 85034-4043
Tel. 602/257-0700
(Other offices in Somerton, Nogales, and Tucson)

Purpose: To provide greater opportunities for constituents to obtain quality and affordable housing, a good education, and meaningful employment; thereby promoting self-sufficiency and dignity for the residents of South Phoenix.
Activity: Publications, human services, community organizing, direct action, public education and training and technical assistance.
Budget: $7,000,000
Employees: Full-time: 250; Part-time: 30; Volunteers: 50; Interns: varies

COMMUNITY ALLIANCE WITH FAMILY FARMERS
P.O. Box 363
Davis, CA 95616
Tel. 916/756-8518
(Other office in San Francisco)

Purpose: To promote sustainable agriculture and provide support to small scale farmers.
Activity: Publications, community organizing, public education and training and technical assistance.
Budget: $630,000
Employees: Full-time: 21; Part-time: 8: Volunteers: 1; Interns: varies

FARMWORKERS ASSOCIATION OF FLORIDA
815 S. Park Avenue
Apopka, FL 32703
Tel. 407/886-5151

Purpose: To build a strong, multi-racial, economically viable organization of farmworkers in Florida, empowering farmworkers to respond to and gain control over the social, political and economic issues affecting their lives.
Activity: Community organizing/advocacy, direct action, public education, research and training and technical assistance.
Budget: $537,360
Employees: Full-time: 19; Part-time: 11; volunteers: 140; Interns: will accept applications

FEDERATION OF SOUTHERN COOPERATIVES
P.O. Box 95
Epes, AL 35460
Tel. 205/652-9676

Purpose: To provide services, resources, and advocacy to over 100 cooperatives and credit unions in the rural South to assist the economic development needs of low-income people.
Activity: Research, lobbying, publications, human services, organizing and training and technical assistance.
Budget: $800,000
Employees: Full-time: 19; Part-time: varies; Interns: varies

INSTITUTE FOR FOOD AND DEVELOPMENT POLICY/FOOD FIRST
398 60th Street
Oakland, CA 94618
Tel. 510/654-4400

Purpose: To empower citizens to solve the problems of hunger, poverty and environmental decline.
Activity: Research, public education, publications.
Budget: $630,000.
Employees: Full-time: 7; Part-time: 1; Volunteers: varies; Interns: varies

NATIONAL COMMUNITY REINVESTMENT COALITION
1875 Connecticut Avenue NW, Suite 1010
Washington, DC 20009
Tel. 202/986-7898

Purpose: To increase access to credit and asset accumulation in low-income, minority and underserved urban and rural communities.
Activity: Research, publications, education, training, technical assistance.
Budget: $380,000
Employees: Full-time: 4; Part-time: 2; Volunteers: 2; Interns: 2

NORTHEAST-MIDWEST INSTITUTE
218 D Street SE
Washington, DC 20003
Tel. 202/544-5200

Purpose: To enhance the economic vitality and environmental quality in the Northeast and Midwest.
Activity: Research and lobbying.
Budget: $1,200,000
Employees: Full-time: 14; Interns: varies

OLDER PERSONS ACTION GROUP, INC.
325 E. Third Avenue, Suite 300
Anchorage, AK 99501
Tel. 907/276-1059
(Other office in Wasilla, AK)

Purpose: To improve services, develop programs, educate, promote and implement changes to foster self-determination of older Alaskan citizens.

Activity: Training and technical assistance, publications, research, direct action and public education.
Budget: $800,000
Employees: Full-time: 24; Part-time: 21; Volunteers: 15; Interns: will accept applications

OREGON FAIR SHARE
306 SE Ash
Portland, OR 97214
Tel. 503/239-7611
(Other offices in Medford, Independence, Eugene, and Salem)

Purpose: To secure greater economic and social justice through nonviolent, grassroots-based citizen action programs.
Activity: Community organizing, public education, direct action, lobbying, research and publications.
Budget: $1,000,000
Employees: Full-time: 23; Part-time: 2; Volunteers: hundreds; Interns: 2

OXFAM AMERICA
26 West Street
Boston, MA 02111
617/482-1211
(Other office in Oakland, CA)

Purpose: To fund locally-generated grassroots development work primarily with peasants in 32 countries.
Activity: Direct action, public education, publications.
Budget: $13,000,000
Employees: Full-time: 60; Part-time: 5; Volunteers: varies; Interns: 5

PARTNERS FOR LIVABLE COMMUNITIES
1429 21st Street NW
Washington, DC 20036
Tel. 202/887-5990

Purpose: To improve communities—their economic health and quality of life—through collaborative resource management.
Activity: Research, education, training, technical assistance, publications.
Budget: $1,400,000
Employees: Full-time: 15; Part-time: 4; Volunteers: varies; Interns: varies

PARTNERSHIP FOR
THE SOUNDS
P.O. Box 55
Columbia, NC 27925
Tel. 919/796-1000
(Other office in Washington, DC)

Purpose: To promote environmental education and sustainable economic development through cultural, historical and nature-based tourism in North Carolina's Albemarle-Pamlico Sounds region.
Activity: Public education, training and technical assistance, community organizing and lobbying.
Budget: $3,000,000
Employees: Full-time: 2; Part-time: 2; Interns: 1

PEOPLE FOR PROGRESS, INC.
301 W. Arkansas Street
Sweetwater, TX 79556
Tel. 915/235-8455

Purpose: To research, develop and operate community service programs that resolve poverty conditions and enable low-income people to become self-sufficient.
Activity: Human services, research, community organizing, direct action, public education and training and technical assistance.
Budget: $5,000,000
Employees: Full-time: 85; Part-time: varies; Volunteers: 5; Interns: 2

WISCONSIN CITIZEN ACTION
152 West Wisconsin Avenue
Suite 308
Milwaukee, WI 53203
Tel. 414/272-2562
(Other offices in Madison, Racine/Kenosha,
Eau Claire, and Green Bay)

Purpose: To fight for social and economic justice at local, state and federal levels.
Activity: Lobbying, public education, community organizing, research and direct action.
Budget: $1,500,000
Employees: Full-time: 47; Part-time: 3; Volunteers: 5; Interns: varies

WOMEN VENTURE
2324 University Avenue
St. Paul, MN 55114
Tel. 612/646-3808

Purpose: To secure a stronger economic future for women through career development, business development and employment programs.
Activity: Training and technical assistance.
Budget: $1,100,000
Employees: Full-time: 18; Part-time: varies; Volunteers: 20; Interns: varies

WOODSTOCK INSTITUTE
407 South Dearborn
Chicago, IL 60605
Tel. 312/427-8070

Purpose: To promote forms of investment in disadvantaged communities that contribute to economic opportunity, community capacity, equity formation and the creation of economically and racially diverse communities.
Activity: Technical assistance, research, program design and publications.
Budget: $617,000
Employees: Full-time: 7; Interns: varies

EDUCATION

Nonprofit organizations focused on education issues are involved in everything from citizenship education to providing educational alternatives to young people and minorities. Compared to many other types of nonprofits, these groups tend to be larger and better financed. The largest in this category, the Close Up Foundation, operates with an annual budget of $34 million and a full-time staff of nearly 200.

ADVOCATES FOR CHILDREN
OF NEW YORK, INC.
24-16 Bridge Plaza South
Long Island City, NY 11101
Tel. 718/729-8866

Purpose: To protect educational entitlements and due process rights of disadvantaged public school children in New York City.
Activity: Case advocacy, public education, training and technical assistance, litigation, research, publications, community organizing.
Budget: $1,000,000
Employees: Full-time: 19; Part-time 4; Volunteers: 3; Interns: 2

ASPIRA ASSOCIATION, INC.
1112 16th Street NW, Suite 340
Washington, DC 20036
Tel. 202/835-3600

Purpose: To empower the Latino Community through education and leadership development of its youth.
Activity: Training and technical assistance, public education, research and publications.
Budget: $1,156,538
Employees: Full-time: 13; Part-time: 2; Volunteers: varies; Interns: 2

CENTER FOR ENVIRONMENTAL EDUCATION
881 Alma Real Drive, Suite 300
Pacific Palisades, CA 90272
Tel. 310/454-4585

Purpose: To collect and make available materials to promote environmental awareness to teachers, students and all who are interested.
Activity: Resource center, research and publications.

Budget: $300,000
Employees: Full-time: 5; Part-time: 1; Volunteers: 10; Interns: 1

CHILDREN'S EXPRESS
30 Cooper Square, 4th Floor
New York, NY 10003
Tel. 212/505-7777
(Other offices in Boston, Indianapolis, New York City,
Oakland, Washington, DC, Australia, and New Zealand)

Purpose: To involve young people in journalism in an attempt to change the way children and teens see and value themselves and are seen and valued by others; to encourage reading, writing and understanding; and to stimulate the child's interest in the world.
Activity: Publications and reporting on children's issues.
Budget: $400,000
Employees: Full-Time: 4; Part-time: 2; Volunteers: 5; Interns: 2

CLOSE UP FOUNDATION
44 Canal Center Plaza
Alexandria, VA 22314
Tel. 703/706-3300

Purpose: To promote citizenship education programs primarily for high school students.
Activity: Educational—primarily through study visits and publications.
Budget: $34,000,000
Employees: Full-time: 180; Part-time: 4; Interns: none, but will accept applications

COMMUNITY ALLIANCE WITH
FAMILY FARMERS
P.O. Box 363
Davis, CA 95616
Tel. 916/756-8518
(Other office in San Francisco)

Purpose: To provide information and technical support to farmers making the transition to ecological farming.
Activity: Publications, community organizing, public education, training and technical assistance.
Budget: $630,000
Employees: Full-time: 21; Part-time: 8; Volunteers: 1; Interns: varies

CONSTITUTIONAL RIGHTS FOUNDATION
601 South Kingsley Drive
Los Angeles, CA 90005
Tel. 213/487-5590

Purpose: To instill in America's youth a deeper understanding of citizenship through values expressed in the Constitution and its Bill of Rights, and educate them to become active and responsible participants in society.
Activity: Training and technical assistance, publications, education.
Budget: $4,000,000
Employees: Full-time: 40; Part-time: 2; Interns: none, but will accept applications

DC SERVICE CORPS
1511 K Street NW, Suite 949
Washington, DC 20005
Tel. 202/347-4136

Purpose: To provide a full-time urban Peace Corps for young people 17-23 years old. Corpsmembers dedicate a year to furthering their education, developing leadership skills, and making a difference in their community through serving others.
Activity: Human services, direct action, training and technical assistance.
Budget: $1,000,000
Employees: Full-time: 18; Volunteers: 3; Interns: varies

DOME PROJECT
486 Amsterdam Avenue
New York, NY 10024
Tel. 212/724-1780

Purpose: To provide educational alternatives and enrichment to youngsters in greatest need—truants, low achievers and court-involved youth.
Activity: Human services, education, training and technical assistance.
Budget: $750,000
Employees: Full-time: 19; Part-time: 10; Volunteers: 12

EAST BAY CONSERVATION CORPS
1021 Third Street
Oakland, CA 94607
Tel. 510/891-3900

Purpose: To promote youth development through community service and service-learning while addressing environmental and social issues.

Activity: Community and human services, education, community organization, training and technical assistance.
Budget: $5,748,588
Employees: Full-time: 64; Part-time: 6; Volunteers: 1500; Interns: 30

EDUCATION LAW CENTER
801 Arch Street
Suite 610
Philadelphia, PA 19107
Tel. 215/238-6970
(Other office in Pittsburgh)

Purpose: To provide quality public education for Pennsylvania students. Focus is pre-school, elementary and secondary education.
Activity: Litigation, case advocacy, public education, training and technical assistance, community organizing.
Budget: $700,000
Employees: Full-time: 9

EDUCATORS FOR SOCIAL RESPONSIBILITY
23 Garden Street
Cambridge, MA 02138
Tel. 617/370-2515
(Other offices in New York, NY; Madison, WI;
Concord, NH; and Carroboro, NC)

Purpose: To help young people develop a commitment to the well-being of others and to make a positive difference in the world.
Activity: Training and technical assistance, publications, and public education.
Budget: $1,200,000
Employees: Full-time: 7: Part-time: 7; Volunteers: varies; Interns: varies

KIDSNET
6856 Eastern Ave. NW, Suite 208
Washington, DC 20012
Tel. 202/291-1400

Purpose: To provide information in print and electronic format for people in the TV industry, educators and parents.
Activity: Publications, research, education, training and technical assistance.
Budget: $250,000
Employees: Full-time: 4; Volunteers: varies; Interns: varies.

LIBRARY THEATRE, INC.
6925 Willow Street, NW
Washington, DC 20012
Tel. 202/291-4800
(Other offices in Bethesda, MD and Hyattsville, MD)

Purpose: To produce theatre and media programs to educate and entertain children and their families on such issues as peer pressure, drug abuse, the importance of hard work in achieving success, and overcoming disabilities and gender stereotypes.
Activity: Public education and publications.
Budget: $350,000
Employees: Full-time: 6; Part-time: varies; Volunteers: 20; Interns: varies

LOS NINOS
287 G Street
Chula Vista, CA 91910
Tel. 619/426-9110
(Other office in Calexico, CA)

Purpose: To improve the quality of life for Mexican children and their families, and to simultaneously provide education on the benefits of self-help community development through cultural interaction.
Activity: Education, training and technical assistance, human services, community organizing, research and publications.
Budget: $500,000
Employees: Full-time: 7; Interns: 2

LULAC NATIONAL EDUCATIONAL SERVICE CENTERS
777 North Capitol Street NE, Suite 305
Washington, DC 20002
Tel. 202/408-0060
(Other offices in Los Angeles, San Francisco, Denver,
Corpus Christi, Chicago, Kansas City, Miami,
Albuquerque, Philadelphia, and Houston)

Purpose: To improve the educational condition of the Hispanic community in the United States by working with business and government to initiate educational programs at the local and national level.
Activity: Human services.
Budget: $2,700,000
Employees: Full-time: 69; Part-time: 11; Volunteers: 20; Interns: 2

NATIONAL ASSOCIATION OF PARTNERS IN EDUCATION
209 Madison Street, Suite 401
Alexandria, VA 22301
Tel. 703/836-4880

Purpose: To provide leadership in the formation and growth of effective partnerships in education that ensure success for all students.
Activity: Training and technical assistance, publications, community organizing, direct action, and public education.
Budget: $1,200,000
Employees: Full-time: 7; Volunteers: 2; Interns: 1

NATIONAL COMMUNITY EDUCATION ASSOCIATION
3929 Old Lee Highway, Suite 91-A
Fairfax, VA 22030
Tel. 703/359-8973

Purpose: To provide the tools and knowledge for lifelong learning; parent and community involvement in education; community use of schools; leadership training for community members and improve the quality of community life through education and training.
Activity: Public education, publications, training and technical assistance.
Budget: $570,000
Employees: Full-time: 4; Part-time: 1; Volunteers: varies; Interns 1

NATIONAL HEAD START ASSOCIATION
201 N. Union Street
Suite 320
Alexandria, VA 22314
Tel. 703/739-0875

Purpose: To nurture and to advocate for children and families; to provide the Head Start community the opportunity of expressing concerns; to define strategies on pertinent issues affecting Head Start; to serve as an advocate for Head Start programs; to provide training and professional development opportunities for the Head Start community; and to develop a networking system with other organizations whose efforts are consistent with the National Head Start Association.
Activity: Research, lobbying, publications, training and technical assistance.
Budget: $2,000,000
Employees: Full-time: 16; Volunteers: varies

NATIONAL INSTITUTE FOR CITIZEN
EDUCATION IN THE LAW
711 G Street SE
Washington, DC 20003
Tel. 202/546-6644

Purpose: To increase citizen understanding of law and the American legal system.
Activity: Training and technical assistance, publications, education.
Budget: $1,200,000
Employees: Full-time: 20; Part-time: 1; Interns: varies

NETWORK, INC.
300 Brickstone Square
Suite 900
Boston, MA 01810
Tel. 508/470-1080
(Other offices in Washington, DC; Burlington, VT; San Juan, PR)

Purpose: To provide support for school improvement efforts; empower clients to achieve their improvement goals; use existing knowledge, research, solutions, and resources toward quality and equity in education.
Activity: Training and technical assistance, human services, research, publications, lobbying for public education.
Budget: $5,000,000
Employees: Full-time: 110; Part-time: 10; Interns: 2

NEW YORK CITY SCHOOL
VOLUNTEER PROGRAM, INC.
443 Park Avenue South
9th Floor
New York, NY 10016
Tel. 212/213-3370

Purpose: To recruit, train and place volunteers as tutors in pre-kindergarten through 12th grade in New York City public schools.
Activity: Public education.
Budget: $1,603,210
Employees: Full-time: 44; Part-time: 17; Volunteers: 12

NOW LEGAL DEFENSE AND
EDUCATION FUND
99 Hudson Street, 12th Floor
New York, NY 10013
Tel. 212/925-6635

Purpose: To advocate legal issues for women and girls.
Activity: Litigation, public education, research, technical assistance.
Budget: $2,200,000
Employees: Full-time: 20; Part-time: 1; Volunteers: 1; Interns: varies

STUDENT COALITION FOR ACTION
IN LITERACY EDUCATION
University of North Carolina
CB #3500
Chapel Hill, NC 27599
Tel. 919/962-1542

Purpose: To mobilize college student involvement with literacy education by assisting college students to start and strengthen their campus-based literacy program.
Activity: Community organizing, public education, training and technical assistance, and publications.
Budget: $350,000
Employees: Full-time: 18; Part-time: 8; Volunteers: varies; Interns: 2

STUDENT PUGWASH USA
1638 R Street NW
Suite 32
Washington, DC 20009
Tel. 202/328-6555

Purpose: To promote concern for the ethical implications of science and technology for students in high school, undergraduate and graduate university level, and professionals.
Activity: Student and public education and publications.
Budget: $400,000
Employees: Full-time: 5; Interns: varies

UNITED STATES STUDENT ASSOCIATION
815 15th Street NW, Suite 838
Washington, DC 20005
Tel. 202/347-8772

Purpose: To lobby for student interests on Capitol Hill and train students on nationwide campuses in techniques of direct action organizing. USSA's overriding goal is student empowerment and increased access to higher education.
Activity: Training and technical assistance, lobbying, membership services, community organizing, publications, direct action, and public education.
Budget: $300,000
Employees: Full-time: 10; Volunteers: 4; Interns: 5

USSA FOUNDATION
815 15th Street, Suite 838
Washington, DC 20005
Tel. 202/347-4768

Purpose: To provide educational materials about USSA's student issue campaigns, to provide technical assistance to campus organizers, to train student activists in Direct Action Organizing.
Activity: Training and technical assistance, public education, community organizing, and publications.
Budget: $200,000
Employees: Full-time: 5; Part-time: 10; Volunteers: 5; Interns: 5

WEST VIRGINIA SCHOLARS ACADEMY
Main & Dogwood Streets
Franklin, WV 26807
Tel. 304/358-2401

Purpose: To raise West Virginia's state college attendance rate by working with motivated disadvantaged students across the state to encourage college attendance and help them formulate strategies for attending college. Obtaining financial aid and gaining admission to appropriate colleges are focuses of this organization.
Activity: Direct action, public education, publications, and research.
Budget: $318,000
Employees: Full-time: 4; Part-time: 3; Volunteers: varies; Interns: None, but will accept applications.

WORK, ACHIEVEMENT, VALUES AND EDUCATION
501 School Street SW
Suite 600
Washington, DC 20024-0183
Tel. 202/484-0103

Purpose: To provide education, job skills training and motivation to economically and educationally disadvantaged youth—usually between the ages of 16 and 24.

Activity: Human services, training and technical assistance, research, lobbying, publications, and direct action.

Budget: $3,200,000

Employees: Full-time: 28; Volunteers: 500; Interns: 2

WORLDTEACH
Harvard Institute for International Development
1 Eliot Street
Cambridge, MA 02138
Tel. 617/495-5527
(Other offices in Ecuador; Poland; Russia; South Africa;
Thailand; China and Nambia)

Purpose: To assist in education and promote cultural exchange, both in the U.S. and abroad by placing university graduates as teachers in developing countries.

Activity: Public education, publications, research, training and technical assistance.

Budget: $514,425

Employees: Full-time: 14; Part-time: 30; Volunteers: 300; Interns: varies

ENVIRONMENT

Environment remains one of the hottest activity areas for nonprofit organizations. Given recent congressional attempts to gut much of the federal environmental legislation as well as downsize the Environmental Protection Agency and the U.S. Department of Interior, environment nonprofits should be very active in the coming months and years. They attract thousands of job seekers who are fervently committed to solving a host of environmental problems. Indeed, within the past 20 years, hundreds of nonprofits have been formed to deal with a large range of environmental issues. Nonprofits are some of the most important organizations for keeping environmental issues at the forefront of public policy debates. Many of these organizations are mass membership groups committed to public education and lobbying at the federal, state, and local levels. Most environmental nonprofits focus on a particular environmental area, such as rivers, oceans, ground water, forests, pollution, nuclear disarmament, wildlife, public lands, or population growth. Many of these nonprofits are small to medium size, but many others are very big with large dues-paying mass memberships. For example, the 1.2 million member National Wildlife Federation operates with an annual budget of $90 million and a staff of 650. The Nature Conservancy operates with an annual budget of over $80 million and a staff of over 800. For more information on jobs with environmental nonprofits, see *Job Opportuniites in the Environment* (Petersons), *Environmental Career Directory* (Visible Ink Press), *Environmental Career Guide* (Wiley), *The New Complete Guide to Environmental Careers* (Island Press) and two directories published by Gale Research: *Gale Environmental Sourcebook* and *World Guide to Environmental Issues*.

1000 FRIENDS OF OREGON
503 SW Third Avenue
Suite 300
Portland, OR 97204
Tel. 503/223-4396

Purpose: To ensure the proper implementation of Oregon's statewide land use laws.
Activity: Litigation, community organizing, training and technical assistance, publications, research, lobbying and public education.

Budget: $900,000
Employees: Full-time: 10; Part-time: 2; Volunteers: varies; Interns: 1

ADIRONDACK COUNCIL, INC.
P.O. Box D-2
Elizabethtown, NY 12932
Tel. 518/873-2240

Purpose: To protect and preserve the Adirondack Park.
Activity: Public education, publications, research, lobbying and litigation.
Budget: $1,500,000
Employees: Full-time: 11; Part-time: 3; Interns: varies

ALASKA CONSERVATION FOUNDATION
430 West Seventh Avenue
Suite 215
Anchorage, AK 99501
907/276-1917

Purpose: To provide financial support and technical assistance to the greater environmental movement in Alaska.
Activity: Grantmaking, training and technical assistance.
Budget: $1,500,000
Employees: Full-time: 3; Part-time: 1; Volunteers: 3

AMERICAN COUNCIL FOR AN ENERGY-EFFICIENT ECONOMY
1001 Connecticut Avenue
Suite 801
Washington, DC 20036
Tel. 202/429-8873
(Other office in Berkeley, CA)

Purpose: To advance energy efficiency as a means of promoting prosperity and environmental protection focusing on national energy policy, efficiency and economic development, utility issues, transportation, buildings, appliances and equipment, industry and international.
Activity: Research, publications, conference organizing, public education, training and technical assistance.
Budget: $1,700,000
Employees: Full-time: 13

AMERICAN FORESTS
1516 P Street NW
Washington, DC 20013
Tel. 202/667-3300

Purpose: To promote and preserve values and benefits of trees and forests in rural and urban areas.
Activity: Direct action, public education, research, publications, training and technical assistance, lobbying, and community organizing.
Budget: $4,000,000
Employees: Full-time: 35; Part-time: 2; Volunteers: 2; Interns: varies

AMERICAN RIVERS
801 Pennsylvania Avenue SE
Suite 400
Washington, DC 20003
Tel. 202/547-6900
(Other offices in Phoenix and Seattle)

Purpose: To preserve and restore America's river systems and foster a river stewardship ethic.
Activity: Litigation, lobbying, direct action, public education, research, community organizing, training and technical assistance.
Budget: $2,400,000
Employees: Full-time: 20; Volunteers: varies; Interns: varies

CALIFORNIA CONSERVATION CORPS
1530 Capitol Avenue
Sacramento, CA 95814
Tel. 916/445-0307

Purpose: To pair two of the state's most precious resources, youth and the environment, to benefit both.
Activity: Provides natural resource work and emergency assistance following natural disasters.
Budget: $50,000,000
Employees: 400 (75 administrative staff; 325 field staff); Part-time: varies; Volunteers: varies

CALIFORNIA PUBLIC INTEREST
RESEARCH GROUP
1147 South Robertson Boulevard
Suite 203
Los Angeles, CA 90035
Tel. 213/278-9244
(Other offices in Berkeley, San Diego, Sacramento,
San Francisco, Santa Cruz, and Santa Barbara)

Purpose: To conduct research and advocate on environmental and consumer issues in California.
Activity: Research, lobbying, litigation, publications, community organizing, and public education.
Budget: $750,000
Employees: Full-time: 62; Part-time: 15; Volunteers: varies; Interns: varies

CENTER FOR MARINE CONSERVATION
1725 DeSales Street NW
Washington, DC 20036
Tel. 202/429-5609
(Other offices in Hampton, VA; St Petersburg, FL;
& San Francisco, CA)

Purpose: To protect the marine environment and its wildlife.
Activity: Research, public education, training and technical assistance, publications, direct action, lobbying and litigation.
Budget: $7,000,000
Employees: Full-time: 35; Part-time: varies; Volunteers: 10; Interns: 4

CHESAPEAKE BAY FOUNDATION
162 Prince George Street
Annapolis, MD 21401
Tel. 301/268-8816
(Other offices in Richmond, VA;
Harrisburg, PA; and Norfolk, VA)

Purpose: To restore and preserve the Chesapeake Bay and its natural resources.
Activity: Direct action, public education, lobbying, litigation, publications and community organizing.
Budget: $6,730,000
Employees: Full-time: 118; Part-time: 9; Volunteers: 250; Interns: varies

CITIZENS ACTION COALITION OF INDIANA
3951 N. Meridian St. #300
Indianapolis, IN 46208
Tel. 317/921-1120
(Other offices in South Bend, Ft. Wayne, and Evansville)

Purpose: To advocate for public interest policies in energy, utility, health care, environment and issues concerning small farmers.
Activity: Research, lobbying, community organizing, public education, litigation, and publications.
Budget: $2,500,000
Employees: Full-time: 85; Part-time: 30; Volunteers: 30; Interns: will accept applications

CITIZENS FOR A BETTER ENVIRONMENT
3255 Hennepin Avenue South
Suite 150
Minneapolis, MN 55408
Tel. 612/824-8537
(Other offices in Milwaukee, WI and Chicago, IL)

Purpose: To protect human and environmental health.
Activity: Public education, community organizing, research, lobbying, litigation, publications, training and technical assistance.
Budget: $1,000,000
Employees: Full-time: 91; Part-time: varies; Volunteers: varies; Interns: varies

CLEAN WATER ACTION
1320 18th Street NW
Suite 300
Washington, DC 20036
Tel. 202/457-1286
(Other offices in Annapolis, MD; Baltimore, MD; Allentown, PA;
Philadelphia, PA; New Brunswick, NJ; Belmar, NJ; Montclair, NJ;
Trenton, NJ; Boston, MA; Amherst, MA; Portsmouth, NH;
Providence, RI; Austin, TX; Denver, CO; Minneapolis, MN;
Rochester, MN; Duluth, MN; Fargo, ND; Lansing, MI;
San Francisco, CA; and Miami, FL)

Purpose: To work for clean and safe water at an affordable cost, control of toxic chemicals, the protection of natural resources and environmental job creation strategies.
Activity: Public education, community organizing, training and technical assistance, research, lobbying, election, publications and direct action.

Budget: $11,000,000
Employees: Full-time: 445; Part-time: 100; Volunteers: varies; Interns: varies

COMMUNITY ENVIRONMENTAL COUNCIL
930 Miramonte Drive
Santa Barbara, CA 93109
Tel. 805/963-0583

Purpose: To conduct environmental research and education.
Activity: Recycling and other operations, public education, research and publications.
Budget: $4,000,000
Employees: Full-time: 40; Part-time: varies; Volunteers: 10; Interns: varies

CONSERVATION LAW FOUNDATION, INC.
62 Summer Street
Boston, MA 02110-1008
Tel. 617/350-0990
(Other offices in Rockland, ME and Montpelier, VT)

Purpose: To confront environmental issues facing the region from courtrooms to town halls. Issues include: conserving natural habitats, open space and agricultural lands, improving urban environments, protecting marine resources, reducing environmental threats to human health, preventing water and air pollution, and developing environmentally sound and economically efficient energy, water use and transportation policies.
Activity: Public education, litigation and publications.
Budget: $2,700,000
Employees: Full-time: 29; Part-time: 8; Volunteers: 9; Interns: varies

COUNCIL ON THE ENVIRONMENT OF NEW YORK CITY
51 Chambers Street, Room 228
New York, NY 10007
Tel. 212/788-7900

Purpose: To promote environmental awareness among New Yorkers and develop solutions to environmental problems.
Activity: Direct action, training and technical assistance and community organizing.
Budget: $2,269,499
Employees: varies

DEFENDERS OF WILDLIFE
1101 14th Street NW
Washington, DC 20005
Tel. 202/659-9510
(Other offices in Sacramento, CA; Missoula, MT; and Portland, OR)

Purpose: To preserve, enhance and protect the natural abundance and diversity of wildlife, including the integrity of natural wildlife ecosystems.
Activity: Research, lobbying, litigation, publications, community organizing, direct action, public education, training and technical assistance.
Budget: $4,500,000
Employees: Full-time: 40; Volunteers: varies; Interns: varies

ENVIRONMENTAL ACTION FOUNDATION
6930 Carroll Avenue, Suite 600
Takoma Park, MD 20912
Tel. 301/891-1100

Purpose: To promote a healthy and sustainable environment.
Activity: Research, public education, organizing, advocacy and litigation.
Budget: $1,100,000
Employees: Full-time: 14; Volunteers: varies; Interns: varies

ENVIRONMENTAL DEFENSE FUND
257 Park Avenue
New York, NY 10010
Tel. 212/505-2100
(Other offices in Boulder, CO; Oakland, CA;
Washington, DC; Raleigh, NC; and Austin, TX)

Purpose: To link science, economics and law to create innovative, economically viable solutions to environmental problems.
Activity: Research, public education, and judicial, administrative and legislative action.
Budget: $18,000,000
Employees: Full-time: 140; Part-time 10; Interns: varies

ENVIRONMENTAL LAW INSTITUTE
1616 P Street NW, Suite 200
Washington, DC 20036
Tel. 202/328-5150

Purpose: To transform laws into action protecting water, air quality, wildlife, and wetlands and reducing public health threats through training,

research and education for communities, governments and businesses.
Activity: Public education, training and technical assistance, publications, community organizing and research.
Budget: $3,000,000
Employees: Full-time: 60; Part-time: 5; Volunteers: 2; Interns: varies

FRIENDS OF THE EARTH
218 D Street SE
Washington, DC 20003
Tel. 202/783-7400
(Other offices in Seattle, WA and Manila, Philippines)

Purpose: To advocate on behalf of global environment issues.
Activity: Lobbying, publications, research, human services, public education, litigation, direct action and community organizing.
Budget: $3,200,000
Employees: Full-time: 35; Part-time: 2; Volunteers: 3

GREENPEACE
1436 U Street NW
Washington, DC 20009
Tel. 202/462-1177
(Other offices in New York, NY; San Francisco, CA;
Seattle, WA; and Chicago, IL)

Purpose: To campaign for toxic waste elimination, nuclear disarmament, protection of marine mammals and the oceans, alternatives to environmentally destructive energy consumption, and prevention of further destruction of the ozone layer.
Activity: Public education, direct action, community organizing, research, lobbying, publications, litigation, training and technical assistance.
Budget: $42,800,000
Employees: Full-time: 175; Part-time: 10; Volunteers: 50; Interns: 25

IN DEFENSE OF ANIMALS
816 W. Francisco Blvd.
San Rafael, CA 94901
Tel. 415/453-9984
(Other offices in San Jose, CA; Richmond, VA;
Shepherdstown, WV; and Greneda, MS)

Purpose: To protect the rights, welfare and habitat of animals by ending the institutionalized exploitation and cruelty to animals.

Activity: Research, community organizing, direct action, public education, lobbying and litigation.
Budget: $1,000,000
Employees: Full-time: 13; Part-time: 5; Volunteers: varies

INFORM, INC.
381 Park Avenue South
New York, NY 10016
Tel. 212/689-4040

Purpose: To identify and report on practical actions for the preservation and conservation of natural resources and public health.
Activity: Research, public education, publications, training and technical assistance.
Budget: $1,654,800
Employees: Full-time: 27; Volunteers: 1; Interns: varies

IZAAK WALTON LEAGUE OF AMERICA
1401 Wilson Blvd., Level B
Arlington, VA 22209
Tel. 703/528-1818
(Other office in Minneapolis, MN)

Purpose: To pursue conservation goals in areas of clean water, acid rain reduction, improve wildlife habitat, protection of natural areas, improvement of outdoor ethics, public land management and farm conservation.
Activity: Research, lobbying, litigation, publications, community organizing and public conservation.
Budget: $1,544,908
Employees: Full-time: 24; Part-time: 1; Interns: varies

LEAGUE OF CONSERVATION VOTERS
1707 L Street NW, Suite 550
Washington, DC 20036
202/785-8683
(Other office in Portsmouth, NH)

Purpose: To help elect pro-environment candidates to the U.S. House of Representatives and Senate.
Activity: Public education, research, publications, development and membership activities.
Budget: $1,000,000
Employees: Full-time: 55; Interns: 5

NATIONAL RECYCLING COALITION, INC.
1101 30th Street NW
Suite 305
Washington, DC 20007
Tel. 202/625-6406

Purpose: To promote recycling.
Activity: Research, community organizing, publications, direct action, training and technical assistance.
Budget: $1,400,000
Employees: Varies

NATIONAL WILDLIFE FEDERATION
1400 16th Street NW
Washington, DC 20036-2266
202/797-6800
(Other Offices in Anchorage, AK; Ann Arbor, MI;
Missoula, MT; Bismarck, ND; Boulder, CO;
Atlanta, GA; Montpelier, VT; Austin, TX; and Portland, OR)

Purpose: To be the nation's most responsible and effective conservation education organization promoting the wise use of natural resources and the protection of the global environment.
Activity: Lobbying, litigation, publications, public education, direct action and research.
Budget: $90,000,000
Employees: Full-time: 650; Part-time: 10; Volunteers: 20; Interns: 40

NATURAL RESOURCES COUNCIL OF MAINE
271 State Street
Augusta, ME 04330-6900
Tel. 207/622-3101

Purpose: To protect, conserve and improve Maine's natural and human environment through advocacy.
Activity: Litigation, research, publications, public education, lobbying, training and technical assistance.
Budget: $1,200,000
Employees: Full-time: 22; Volunteers: varies; Interns: 2

NATURE CONSERVANCY
1815 North Lynn Street
Arlington, VA 22209
Tel. 703/841-5300

Purpose: To preserve global biological diversity—rare plants, animals and natural communities.
Activity: Protection, fundraising, stewardship, research and publications.
Budget: $81,700,000
Employees: Full-time: 831; Part-time: 94; Volunteers: low 100,000's; Interns: varies

NORTHEAST-MIDWEST INSTITUTE
218 D Street SE
Washington, DC 20003
Tel. 202/544-5200

Purpose: To enhance the economic vitality and environmental quality.
Activity: Research and lobbying.
Budget: $1,200,000
Employees: Full-time: 14; Interns: varies

PENNSYLVANIA ENVIRONMENTAL COUNCIL
1211 Chestnut Street, Suite 900
Philadelphia, PA 19130
Tel. 215/563-0275

Purpose: To advocate for environmental legislation and regulation and educate citizens of Pennsylvania about the importance of these measures.
Activity: Research, lobbying, publications, community organizing, direct action, public education, training and technical assistance.
Budget: $900,000
Employees: Full-time: 12; Part-time: 5; Volunteers: varies; Interns: varies

RAINFOREST ALLIANCE
65 Bleecker Street
New York, NY 10012
Tel. 212/677-1900

Purpose: To conserve the world's endangered tropical forests.
Activity: Research projects, education, publications.
Budget: $2,000,000
Employees: Full-time: 25; Part-time: 9; Volunteers: 20; Interns: varies

ROCKY MOUNTAIN INSTITUTE
1739 Snowmass Creek Road
Old Snowmass, CO 81654
Tel. 303/927-3851

Purpose: To foster the efficient and sustainable use of resources as a path to global security. Program areas include energy, water, agriculture, economic renewal and energy security, transportation and Green Development services.
Activity: Research, technical assistance, public education, publication of research findings, direct action and community organizing.
Budget: $1,929,853
Employees: Full-time: 32; Part-time: 10; Volunteers: varies; Interns: varies

SIERRA CLUB
730 Polk Street
San Francisco, CA 94109
Tel. 415/776-2211
(Other offices in Washington, DC; Saratoga Springs, NY;
Annapolis, MD; Birmingham, AL; Madison, WI; Sheridan. WY;
Dallas, TX; Boulder, CO; Phoenix, AZ; Salt Lake City, UT;
Los Angeles, CA; Oakland, CA; Seattle, WA; Anchorage, AK;
and North Palm Beach, FL)

Purpose: To explore, enjoy and protect the wild places of the earth; to practice and promote the responsible use of the earth's ecosystems and resources; to educate and enlist humanity to protect and restore the quality of the natural and human environment; and to use all lawful means to carry out these objectives.
Activity: Research, lobbying, publications, community organizing, education.
Budget: $35,000,000
Employees: Full-time: 375; Part-time: varies; Volunteers: varies; Interns: varies

TRUST FOR PUBLIC LAND
116 New Montgomery, 4th Floor
San Francisco, CA 94105
Tel. 415/495-4014
(Other offices in Washington, DC; Norwich, VT; Sacramento, CA;
Austin, TX: Costa Mesa, CA; Los Angeles; New York;
Morristown, NJ; Minneapolis; Boston; Tallahassee, FL;
Atlanta; South Miami, FL; Santa Fe, NM; Seattle; Portland, OR)

Purpose: To conserve land for people to enjoy.
Activity: Research, lobbying, litigation, publications, public education, training and technical assistance, land acquisition and Open space financing.

Budget: $18,000,000
Employees: Full-time: 180; Part-time: varies; Interns: varies

WOODLANDS MOUNTAIN INSTITUTE
Main & Dogwood Streets
Franklin, WV 26807
Tel. 304/358-2401
(Other offices in Kathmandu, Nepal and Shigalee, Tibet)

Purpose: To advance mountain cultures and preserve mountain environments worldwide.
Activity: Direct action, human services, research, training and technical assistance and membership development.
Budget: $1,500,000
Employees: Full-time: 50; Part-time: 3

WORLD RESOURCES INSTITUTE
1709 New York Avenue NW, 7th Floor
Washington, DC 20006
Tel. 202/638-6300

Purpose: To provide accurate information about global resources and environmental conditions, analyze emerging issues, and develop creative yet workable policy responses.
Activity: Research, publications, outreach on research and publications, training and technical assistance and public education.
Budget: $8,500,000
Employees: Full-time: 85; Interns: varies

WORLD WILDLIFE FUND/
THE CONSERVATION FOUNDATION
1250 24th Street NW
Washington, DC 20037
Tel. 202/293-4800
(Other office in Gland, Switzerland)

Purpose: To protect endangered wildlife and wildlands especially in the tropical forests of Latin America, Asia and Africa. A mass membership organization with 1.2 members.
Activity: Training and technical assistance, direct action, research, community organizing, publications, human services and public education.
Budget: $60,000,000
Employees: N/A (600+)

WORLDWATCH INSTITUTE
1776 Massachusetts Avenue NW
Washington, DC 20036
Tel. 202/452-1999

Purpose: To alert policymakers and the general public to emerging global trends in the availability and management of resources, both human and natural.
Activity: Research and publications.
Budget: $2,500,000
Employees: Full-time: 30; Part-time: 1

ZERO POPULATION GROWTH
1400 16th Street NW, Suite 320
Washington, DC 20036
Tel. 202/332-2200
(Other office in Los Angeles, CA)

Purpose: To achieve a sustainable balance of population, resources and the environment—both in the United States and worldwide.
Activity: Research, lobbying, publications, community organizing, public education, training and technical assistance.
Budget: $2,500,000
Employees: Full-time: 25; Part-time: 3; Volunteers: 3; Interns: varies

FOOD AND NUTRITION

Food and nutrition are important activities for numerous nonprofit organizations. Some of the largest nonprofit organizations primarily deal with these issues in Third and Fourth World countries (see Chapter 9 for additional listings). However, some nonprofits focus on food and nutrition issues in the United States. Most of these organizations are relatively small with annual budgets under $2 million and with staffs under 15 employees.

BREAD FOR THE CITY
1525 7th Street NW
Washington, DC 20001
Tel. 202/332-0440

Purpose: To provide emergency food, clothing and social services to low-income residents of the District of Columbia.
Activity: Human services, training and technical assistance, and lobbying.
Budget: $850,000
Employees: Full-time: 14; Part-time: 3; Volunteers: 70; Interns: varies

BREAD FOR THE WORLD
1100 Wayne Avenue, Suite 1000
Silver Spring, MD 20910
Tel. 301/608-2400
(Other offices in Minneapolis, Chicago and Los Angeles)

Purpose: To help the world's hungry by lobbying U.S. decision-makers.
Activity: Research, publications, community organizing, public education, and lobbying by members.
Budget: $2,600,000
Employees: Full-time: 42; Part-time: 5; Volunteers: 22; Interns: 8

CENTER FOR SCIENCE IN THE PUBLIC INTEREST
1875 Connecticut Avenue NW
Suite 300
Washington, DC 20009
Tel. 202/332-9110

Purpose: To conduct research, educate and advocate about nutrition, diet, food safety, alcohol and related food issues.

Activity: Public education, supporting services, publications, research, litigation, and lobbying.
Budget: $12,000,000
Employees: Full-time: 35; Part-time: 1; Volunteers: 1; Interns: varies

COMMUNITY FOOD RESOURCE CENTER
90 Washington Street
New York, NY 10006
Tel. 212/349-8155

Purpose: To increase access to nutritious food at reasonable cost for all New Yorkers—especially families and individuals living in poverty.
Activity: Public education, human services, community organizing, publications, direct action, training and technical assistance.
Budget: $1,800,000
Employees: Full-time: 46; Part-time: varies; Interns: will accept applications

FOOD RESEARCH AND ACTION CENTER
1875 Connecticut Ave. NW, Suite 540
Washington, DC 20009
Tel. 202/986-2200

Purpose: To end hunger and malnutrition in the United States.
Activity: Research, lobbying, litigation, publications, organizing, public education, training and technical assistance.
Budget: $1,200,000
Employees: Full-time: 18; Part-time: varies; Interns: varies

SHARE OUR STRENGTH
1511 K Street NW
Suite 623
Washington, DC 20005
Tel. 202/393-2925

Purpose: To raise funds (working primarily through the restaurant industry) and awareness for the relief of hunger, homelessness and illiteracy in the U.S. and overseas.
Activity: Grants program through which funds are distributed to public education, community organizing, publications, and research.
Budget: $1,085,000
Employees: Full-Time: 6; Volunteers: 6; Interns: will accept applications

HOUSING AND THE HOMELESS

Housing and the homeless represent important social issues for hundreds of nonprofit organizations. Nonprofits focusing on these issues deal with tenants rights, housing discrimination, community development, employment, minorities, construction, neighborhood preservation, legal services, ex-offenders, and shelter. While most of these organizations are community-based and relatively small in size, some, such as Habitat for Humanity, are relatively large and have a national and international presence. Nonprofits working in these areas tend to be heavily involved in providing direct services to the poor and homeless.

ASIAN COUNSELING AND REFERRAL SERVICE
1032 S. Jackson Street
Suite 200
Seattle, WA 98104
Tel. 206/461-3606
(Other office in Bellevue, WA)

Purpose: To provide and advocate for human services to empower Asian and Pacific Islander individuals and communities to obtain social and economic well being.
Activity: Human services, public education, community organizing, direct action, training and technical assistance.
Budget: $3,100,000
Employees: Full-time: 45; Volunteers: varies; Interns: varies

BALTIMORE NEIGHBORHOODS, INC.
2217 Saint Paul Street
Baltimore, MD 21218
Tel. 410/243-6007

Purpose: To promote justice in housing, advocate tenants rights, and eliminate illegal discrimination.
Activity: Litigation, direct action, human services, and community organizing.
Budget: $300,000
Employees: Full-time: 10; Volunteers: 100

CENTER FOR COMMUNITY CHANGE
1000 Wisconsin Avenue NW
Washington, DC 20007
Tel. 202/342-0519
(Other office in San Francisco)

Purpose: To help poor Americans help themselves by building strong community organizations, help them create jobs, build affordable housing, raise money and develop effective community programs.
Activity: Training and technical assistance, research and development, public policy, research, publications, and lobbying.
Budget: $4,000,000
Employees: Full-time: 42; Part-time: 3; Interns: varies

CHICANOS POR LA CAUSA, INC.
1112 East Buckeye Road
Phoenix, AZ 85034-4043
Tel. 602/257-0700
(Other offices in Somerton, AZ; Nogales, AZ; and Tucson, AZ)

Purpose: To provide greater opportunities for constituents to obtain quality and affordable housing, education, and meaningful employment.
Activity: Publications, human services, community organizing, direct action, public education, training and technical assistance.
Budget: $7,000,000
Employees: Full-time: 250; Part-time: 30; Volunteers: 50; Interns: varies

COALITION FOR THE HOMELESS
1234 Massachusetts Avenue, Suite C 1015
Washington, DC 20005
Tel. 202/374-8870

Purpose: To help the homeless regain self-sufficiency and independence.
Activity: Human services.
Budget: $2,500,000
Employees: Full-time: 53; Part-time: 15; Volunteers: 100; Interns: 10

FRIENDLY HOUSE, INC.
802 S. 1st Avenue
Phoenix, AZ 85030
Tel. 602/257-1870

Purpose: To assist those seeking to enter the mainstream of American life.
Activity: Human services, public education and research.

Budget: $2,800,000
Employees: Full-time: 55; Part-time: 60; Volunteers: 15; Interns: will accept applications

GOOD SHEPHERD HOUSING AND FAMILY SERVICES, INC.
6301 Richmond Highway
Alexandria, VA 22306
Tel. 703/765-9407

Purpose: To help low-income families/individuals and those in crisis obtain and keep decent, affordable housing.
Activity: Human services and direct action, community organizing, research, lobbying, public education and publications.
Budget: $800,000
Employees: Full-time: 6; Part-time: 2; Volunteers: 50; Interns 1

HABITAT FOR HUMANITY INTERNATIONAL
121 Habitat Street
Americas, GA 31709-3498
Tel. 912/924-6935

Purpose: To eliminate poverty from the world and make decent housing a matter of conscience and action.
Activity: Direct action, human services, public education and publications.
Budget: $21,000,000
Employees: Full-time: 70; Part-time: varies: Volunteers: 100; Interns: varies

HOUSING AND CREDIT COUNSELING, INC.
1195 SW Buchanan, Suite 203
Topeka, KS 66604-1183
Tel. 913/234-0217
(Other offices in Lawrence, KS and Manhattan, KS)

Purpose: To facilitate safe, adequate, affordable and equitable housing situations for all people—particularly those of low and moderate income and to assist with budgeting and debt repayment alternatives.
Activity: Human services, public education, training and technical assistance, and community organizing.
Budget: $500,000
Employees: Full-time: 21; Part-time: 1; Volunteers: varies; Interns: 2

HOUSING ASSISTANCE COUNCIL
1025 Vermont Avenue NW, Suite 606
Washington, DC 20005
Tel. 202/842-8600
(Other offices in Atlanta, GA; Mill Valley, CA; Albuquerque, NM)

Purpose: To assist in the provision of decent, sanitary, affordable housing for the rural poor.
Activity: Training, technical assistance, direct action, research, publications.
Budget: $2,000,000
Employees: Full-time: 25; Interns: 2

HOUSING ASSOCIATION OF DELAWARE VALLEY
1314 Chestnut Street, Suite 900
Philadelphia, PA 19107
Tel. 215/545-6010

Purpose: To end racism and exploitation in housing and ensure decent housing for all residents of the Delaware Valley regardless of race or income.
Activity: Research, publications, public education, training and technical assistance, housing counseling and housing development.
Budget: $2,790,000
Employees: Full-time: 12; Interns: varies

ILLINOIS TENANTS UNION
4616 North Drake
Chicago, IL 60625
Tel. 312/478-1133

Purpose: To provide legal advice and representation to tenants.
Activity: Public education and litigation.
Budget: $200,000
Employees: Full-time: 8; Part-time: 8 contract attorneys; Volunteers: varies; Interns: will accept applications

IT'S TIME...INC.
139 Henry Street
New York, NY 10002
Tel. 212/962-3069

Purpose: To empower low-income residents of the Lower East Side through tenant organizing, the preservation and development of low-income housing and social services to youth and senior citizens.

Activity: Community organizing, human services, training and technical assistance.
Budget: $240,000
Employees: Full-time: 10; Part-time: 5; Volunteers: 3; Interns: varies

LAWYERS ALLIANCE FOR NEW YORK
99 Hudson Street
New York, NY 10013
Tel. 212/219-1800

Purpose: To promote low-income housing development and neighborhood preservation and provide legal services to nonprofit organizations.
Activity: Training and technical assistance, publications, direct action, fundraising and volunteer placement.
Budget: $1,000,000
Employees: Full-time: 16; Part-time: 2; Volunteers: 1; Interns: 3

MASSACHUSETTS COALITION FOR THE HOMELESS
288 A Street
Boston, MA 02210
Tel. 617/737-3508
(Other office in Worcester, MA)

Purpose: To initiate and support public policies concerning housing, income maintenance programs, job and training programs, medical and mental health care and legal rights and services.
Activity: Direct services, lobbying, research, litigation, publications, human services, community organizing and public education.
Budget: $550,000
Employees: Full-time: 11; Volunteers; 150; Interns: varies

MASSACHUSETTS HALF-WAY HOUSES, INC.
Back Bay Annex, P.O. Box 348
Boston, MA 02117
Tel. 617/437-1864

Purpose: To provide residential and non-residential support services to ex-offenders with the goal of achieving successful reintegration into the community after incarceration.
Activity: Human services, training and technical assistance.
Budget: $4,500,000
Employees: Full-time: 118; Volunteers: 50; Interns: varies

NATIONAL COALITION FOR
THE HOMELESS
1621 K Street NW, Suite 1004
Washington, DC 20006
Tel. 202/775-1322
(Other office in New York City)

Purpose: To address and end homelessness through a multi-level strategy of securing rights, services and housing for homeless people.
Activity: Lobbying, research, litigation, publications, human services, community organizing, direct action, public education, training and technical assistance.
Budget: $550,000
Employees: Full-time: 8; Part-time: 2; Volunteers: 5; Interns: varies

PROJECT NOW COMMUNITY
ACTION AGENCY
418 19th Street
P.O. Box 3970
Rock Island, IL 61201
Tel. 309/793-6391
(Other offices in Moline, Kewanee, Aledo, and East Miline, IL)

Purpose: To develop, mobilize, and utilize to the maximum extent possible all available human and material resources on the local, state, and national levels for the purpose of combating and eliminating poverty.
Activity: Human services, training and technical assistance, public education, and community organizing.
Budget: $4,800,000
Employees: Full-time: 150; Part-time: 55; Volunteers: 100; Interns: 10

URBAN HOMESTEADING
ASSISTANCE, INC.
40 Prince Street, 2nd Floor
New York, NY 10012
Tel. 212/226-4119

Purpose: To provide technical assistance to low-income tenants associations and cooperatives in New York City and nationally.
Activity: Training and technical assistance, publications, community organizing, research and public education.
Budget: $1,000,000
Employees: Full-time: 31; Part-time: 3; Volunteers: varies; Interns: varies

MEDICAL AND HEALTH CARE

Medical and health care nonprofits focus on a wide range of health issues, from mental health, cancer, and family planning to AIDS, minority health care, and the handicapped. Each major disease or medical problem area tends to have its own set of nonprofit organizations supporting research and education and providing technical assistance and direct services. Many of these groups lobby for changes in government health care policies.

During the past few years, numerous nonprofit organizations have formed throughout the country to deal with HIV/AIDS. Many of these groups are now well financed, having been successful in getting funding from foundations and federal, state, and local governments. Others continue to struggle for basic funding to support their services.

The organizations represented in this section primarily focus on health issues in the United States. Some of the largest organizations dealing with medical and health issues, especially those dealing with family planning, eye care, and medical relief, are international nonprofits. We identify and profile many of these international nonprofits in Chapter 9.

ACTION ON SMOKING AND HEALTH
2013 H Street NW
Washington, DC 20006
Tel. 202/659-4310

Purpose: To promote and take legal action for nonsmokers' rights.
Activity: Litigation, public education, publications, research.
Budget: $1,000,000
Employees: Full-time: 9; Part-time: 1; Interns: 2

AIDS ACTION COUNCIL
1875 Connecticut Avenue NW, Suite 700
Washington, DC 20009
Tel. 202/986-1300

Purpose: To lobby the federal government on behalf of AIDS communities.
Activity: Lobbying, community organizing, media relations, publications.
Budget: $2,000,000
Employees: Full-time: 20; Part-time: 3; Volunteers: varies; Interns: 2

AIDS FOUNDATION OF CHICAGO
411 S. Wells
Chicago, IL 60607
Tel. 312/642-5454

Purpose: To coordinate activities of local agencies committed to AIDS care and prevention and advocate for policies and increased public funding.
Activity: Lobbying, grantmaking, community organizing, training and technical assistance.
Budget: $4,000,000
Employees: Full-time: 16; Part-time: 2; Volunteers: 4; Interns: 1

AIDS PROJECT—LOS ANGELES
1313 N. Vine Street
Los Angeles, CA 90028
Tel. 213/993-1600

Purpose: To provide HIV/AIDS services and information and advocate at all levels of government for people with HIV/AIDS.
Activity: Lobbying, publications, community organizing, public education, training and technical assistance.
Budget: $19,000,000.
Employees: Full-time: 220; Part-time: 20; Volunteers: 2500; Interns: varies

AMERICAN INDIAN HEALTH SERVICE OF CHICAGO
838 West Irving Park Road
Chicago, IL 60613
Tel. 312/883-9100

Purpose: To increase financial and cultural accessibility to health and human services for American Indians.
Activity: Human services, community development, educational advocacy, research, publications, public education, and training and technical assistance.
Budget: $300,000
Employees: Full-time: 14; Part-time: 5; Volunteers: 4; Interns: varies

AMERICAN LUNG ASSOCIATION
1740 Broadway
New York, NY 10019-4374
Tel. 212/315-8700

Purpose: To fight lung disease and promote healthy lungs.
Activity: Research, lobbying, publications, human services, community

organizing, direct action, public education/management, training and technical assistance, and professional education.
Budget: Each state, DC, Puerto Rico and the Virgin Islands have lung associations. Each is separately incorporated and does its own recruiting and hiring. Budgets range in size from less than $200,000 to over $2 million.
Employees: Full-time: 1500 nationwide; Part-time: varies; Volunteers: varies; Interns: varies

AMERICAN SOCIAL HEALTH ASSOCIATION
100 Capitola Drive
Durham, NC 27713
Tel. 919/361-8400
(Other office in Washington, DC)

Purpose: To stop sexually transmitted disease.
Activity: Public education; research, lobbying, publications, training and technical assistance.
Budget: $8,856,000
Employees: Full-time: 100; Part-time: 206; Volunteers: 9; Interns: will accept applications

BOSTON WOMEN'S HEALTH
BOOK COLLECTIVE
240 A Elm Street
Somerville, MA 02144-2935
Tel. 617/625-0277

Purpose: Women's health education, advocacy and activism.
Activity: Public education, training and technical assistance, publications, research, community organizing, direct action, and litigation.
Budget: $250,000
Employees: Full-time: 13; Part-time: 3; Volunteers: 5

CITIZENS FOR BETTER CARE
2111 Woodward Avenue, Suite 610
Detroit, MI 48226
Tel. 313/962-5968
(Other Michigan offices in Lansing, Grand Rapids, Saginaw,
Traverse City, and Iron Mountain)

Purpose: To help people with the selection of/or who have problems with nursing homes, homes for the aged or other long-term health care services.
Activity: Handling consumer complaints and requests for information, developing issue papers, monitoring state and federal action, public education,

training and technical assistance, publications and lobbying.
Budget: $1,200,000
Employees: Full-time: 30; Part-time: 5; Volunteers: 50; Interns: 3

CONCORD FEMINIST HEALTH CENTER
38 South Main Street
Concord, NH 03307
Tel. 603/225-2739

Purpose: To provide health care to women in a feminist model.
Activity: Human services; publications, public education, direct action, lobbying, and community organizing.
Budget: $750,000
Employees: Full-time: 16; Interns: varies

EAST COAST MIGRANT HEALTH PROJECT
1234 Massachusetts Avenue NW
Suite 623
Washington, DC 20005
Tel. 202/347-7377

Purpose: To provide health and allied-health professionals to supplement existing staff at community health centers on the East Coast. Assists in the delivery of health and social services to migrant/seasonal farmworkers and their families. Staff move twice a year to serve during the harvest seasons.
Activity: Human services, public education, training and technical assistance.
Budget: $695,000
Employees: Full-time: 18 in winter, 35 in summer; Volunteers: varies; Interns: 1

ENVIRONMENTAL HEALTH COALITION
1717 Kettner Blvd.
Suite 100
San Diego, CA 92101
Tel. 619/235-0281

Purpose: To prevent illness and environmental degradation resulting from exposure to toxins in the home, workplace and community.
Activity: Public education, training and technical assistance, research, community organizing, and direct action.
Budget: $300,000
Employees: Full-time: 9; Part-time: 3; Volunteers: varies; Interns: varies

HEALTH CARE FOR ALL
30 Winter Street, Suite 1007
Boston, MA 02108
Tel. 617/350-7279

Purpose: To promote reform of the health care system on both state and national levels and operate a health care information helpline.
Activity: Community organizing, public education, human services, research, publications, lobbying, direct action, and litigation.
Budget: $400,000
Employees: Full-time: 8; Part-time: 2; Volunteers: 10; Interns: 6

HEALTH CRISIS NETWORK
5050 Biscayne Blvd.
Miami, FL 33134
Tel. 305/751-7775

Purpose: To provide counseling and support services, public information and education in response to HIV spectrum illness for the greater Miami area.
Activity: Human services, public education, training and technical assistance.
Budget: $3,100,000
Employees: Full-time: 54; Part-time: 20; Volunteers: 500; Interns: varies

LA FRONTERA CENTER, INC.
502 West 29th Street
Tucson, AZ 85713
Tel. 602/884-9920

Purpose: To provide a network of accessible, coordinated, mental health, vocational rehabilitation and chemical dependency services that are responsive and relevant to the needs of a culturally diverse community.
Activity: Human services and public education.
Budget: $11,000,000
Employees: Full-time: 250; Part-time: varies: Volunteers: varies; Interns: varies

LEE COUNTY COOPERATIVE CLINIC
530 West Atkins Boulevard
Marianna, AR 72360
Tel. 501/295-5225
(Other offices in Madison and Lakeview)

Purpose: To deliver out-patient medical care to residents of Lee County at affordable prices.

Activity: Human services, community organizing, lobbying, and research.
Budget: $1,500,000
Employees: Full-time: 50; Part-time: 5; Volunteers: 1

LOS ANGELES REGIONAL FAMILY PLANNING COUNCIL, INC.
3600 Wilshire Boulevard, Suite 600
Los Angeles, CA 90010
Tel. 213/386-5614

Purpose: To provide fiscal monitoring, quality assurance, training, data processing and other services to delegate agencies to increase the accessibility and availability of reproductive health services to all persons regardless of income.
Activity: Research, human services, public relations, public education, training and technical assistance.
Budget: $20,000,000
Employees: Full-time: 46; Part-time: 2; Volunteers: 6; Interns: occasionally

MEDICARE ADVOCACY PROJECT, INC.
520 S. Lafayette Park Place
Suite 214
Los Angeles, CA 90057
Tel. 213/383-4519

Purpose: To assist seniors in Los Angeles County with Medicare and related health care problems/issues.
Activity: Direct action, education, lay advocate training and supervision, litigation, training and technical assistance, research and publications.
Budget: $700,000
Employees: Full-time: 14; Part-time: 2; Volunteers: 60; Interns: varies

NATIONAL ABORTION FEDERATION
1436 U Street NW, Suite 103
Washington, DC 20008
Tel. 202/667-5881

Purpose: To enhance the quality and accessibility of abortion care.
Activity: Public education, training and technical assistance, publications, human services, research, health care services-legal clearinghouse, and guidance on response to violence.
Budget: $1,000,000
Employees: Full-time: 13; Part-time: 1; Interns: 2

NATIONAL AIDS NETWORK
2033 M Street NW
Suite 800
Washington, DC 20036
Tel. 202/293-2437

Purpose: To provide leadership, information, and support to community-based AIDS education and service providers.
Activity: Public education, training and technical assistance, community organizing, and publications.
Budget: $1,400,000
Employees: Full-time: 17; Part-time: 3; Interns: varies

NATIONAL ALLIANCE FOR
THE MENTALLY ILL
2101 Wilson Boulevard, Suite 302
Arlington, VA 22201
Tel. 703/524-7600

Purpose: To provide emotional support and information on the biological nature of serious mental illness through local family support groups, advocate for better treatment and community services, promote research on causes and treatments of serious mental illness, and seek to eliminate the stigma associated with these disorders.
Activity: An alliance of self-help/advocacy groups in all 50 states. Public education, training and technical assistance, human services, publications, lobbying, and direct action.
Budget: $3,000,000
Employees: Full-time: 35; Part-time: 2; Volunteers: 30; Interns: varies

NATIONAL BLACK WOMEN'S
HEALTH PROJECT
1237 Ralph David Abernathy Blvd., SW
Atlanta, GA 30310
Tel. 404/758-9590
(Other office in Washington, DC)

Purpose: To provide wellness education and services, self-help group development, and health information and advocacy in order to reduce the health care problems amongst black women and their families.
Activities: 26 state groups and 150 local groups. Public education, community organizing and publications.
Budget: $1,600,000
Employees: Full-time: 19; Part-time: 2: Volunteers: 10; Interns: varies

NATIONAL MINORITY AIDS COUNCIL
300 Eye Street NE
Suite 400
Washington, DC 20002
Tel. 202/544-1076

Purpose: To develop and guide national public policy initiatives on HIV/AIDS infection in communities of color and serve as a clearinghouse for information on AIDS affecting minority communities.
Activity: Lobbying, publications, community organizing, public education, research, training and technical assistance, and conferences.
Budget: $12,000,000
Employees: Full-time: 20; Part-time: 1; Interns: 1

NATIONAL NATIVE AMERICAN AIDS PREVENTION CENTER
3515 Grand Avenue
Suite 100
Oakland, CA 94610
Tel. 510/444-2051
(Other offices in Minneapolis, MN and Oklahoma City, OK)

Purpose: To support community efforts in Native communities by providing education and information services and training/technical assistance as well as provide case management and client advocacy services to Native Americans with HIV infection.
Activity: Training and technical assistance, publications, case management.
Budget: $2,000,000.
Employees: Full-time: 16; Part-time: 2

OPERATION CONCERN
1853 Market Street
San Francisco, CA 94103
Tel. 415/626-7000

Purpose: To provide mental health and social services to the lesbian and gay community in a multicultural environment, with attention to youth, elders, the disabled, couples and families and substance abusers.
Activity: Human services, training, technical assistance, education.
Budget: $900,000
Employees: Full-time: 26; Part-time: 16; Volunteers: 35; Interns: 13

PLANNED PARENTHOOD FEDERATION
810 Seventh Avenue
New York, NY 10019
Tel. 212/541-7800

Purpose: To provide leadership in promoting voluntary fertility decisions, including contraception, abortion, sterilization, and infertility services.
Activity: Operates 900 centers delivering reproductive health services and educational programs. Human services, lobbying, litigation, public education, community organizing, research, training and technical assistance.
Budget: $405,000,000
Employees: Full-time: 10,068; Part-time: 2; Interns: 1

PUBLIC CITIZEN'S HEALTH RESEARCH GROUP
2000 P Street NW
Suite 700
Washington, DC 20036
Tel. 202/833-3000

Purpose: To promote the public's health by monitoring the work of the medical establishment, the drug industry and the health related regulatory agencies as well as writing and distributing publications that help give consumers more control over their health decisions.
Activity: Research, lobbying, publications, direct action and public education.
Budget: $600,000
Employees: Full-time: 8; Part-time: varies; Volunteers: varies

SAN FRANCISCO AIDS FOUNDATION
25 Van Ness Avenue
6th Floor
San Francisco, CA 94102
Tel. 415/864-5855

Purpose: To provide direct services to people with AIDS and HIV by helping to educate the public to prevent transmission of HIV; helping individuals make informed choices about treatment options and other AIDS-related concerns; protecting the dignity and human rights of those affected by HIV; and initiating and supporting public policies to further these goals.
Activity: Lobbying, publications, human services, community organizing, direct action, public education, training and technical assistance.
Budget: $8,800,000
Employees: Full-time: 88; Part-time: 2; Volunteers: 500; Interns: varies

POLITICAL AND
GOVERNMENT REFORM

Much of what nonprofit organizations do is aimed at influencing government policy. Whether the issues are housing, education, health care, or environment, the methods and goals are often the same— lobby government decision-makers.

Numerous nonprofit organizations are organized specifically to influence government. Some of these groups, such as policy institutes and think tanks, conduct studies and present their findings to government officials. Others, like The Urban Institute, operate similarly to private contractors—receive contracts and grants to do government-sponsored research on important public policy issues. And still others, like the National Women's Political Caucus, support pro-choice women for political office.

Nonprofit organizations in this category range from very small operations to large public policy institutes. They represent both conservative and liberal groups. Common Cause, which has a great deal of public visibility, operates with an annual budget of nearly $12 million and with a full-time staff of 60. Conservative think tanks, such as the Hoover Institution ($20 million), American Enterprise Institute ($12 million), and the Heritage Foundation ($20 million), operate with relatively large budgets and staffs. More liberal think tanks, such as The Brookings Institution ($20 million) and The Urban Institute ($21 million), are similar in size.

If you are passionately committed to particular public policy issues or love to work with public policy issues, this group of nonprofit organizations may be an ideal "fit" for you.

AIDS ACTION COUNCIL
1875 Connecticut Ave. NW, Suite 700
Washington, DC 20009
Tel. 202/986-1300

Purpose: To lobby the federal government to develop federal HIV/AIDS policies to increase AIDS research and improve treatment and prevention.
Activity: Lobbying, community organizing, media relations and publications.
Budget: $1,500,000
Employees: Full-time: 21; Part-time: 3; Volunteers: varies; Interns: 2

ARIZONA CENTER FOR LAW
IN THE PUBLIC INTEREST
3724 N. Third Street, Suite 300
Phoenix, AZ 85012
602/274-6287
(Other office in Tucson, AZ)

Purpose: To provide an effective voice for individuals and groups that otherwise would be unable to obtain effective legal representation.
Activity: Research, lobbying, litigation, education, training and technical assistance.
Budget: $900,000
Employees: Full-time: 21; Part-time: 1; Volunteers: 4; Interns: varies

CENTER FOR POLICY ALTERNATIVES
1875 Connecticut Avenue NW, Suite 710
Washington, DC 20009
Tel. 202/387-6030

Purpose: To serve as a policy resource organization specializing in innovation and reform by America's state governments.
Activity: Research, organizing, education, training and technical assistance.
Budget: $1,200,000
Employees: Full-time: 25; Part-time: 3; Interns: varies

CITIZEN ACTION OF LOUISIANA
7434 Picardy Avenue, Suite D
Baton Rouge, LA 70809
Tel. 504/769-8896

Purpose: To gain community empowerment through the passage of progressive consumer legislation.
Activity: Research, lobbying, community organizing and public education.
Budget: $400,000
Employees: Full-time: 14; Part-time: 4; Volunteers: 1

CITIZENS ACTION COALITION OF INDIANA
3951 N. Meridian St. #300
Indianapolis, IN 46208
Tel. 317/921-1120
(Other offices in South Bend, Ft. Wayne, and Evansville)

Purpose: To advocate in areas of energy policy, utility policy, health care policy, environmental policy and issues concerning small farmers.

Activity: Research, lobbying, community organizing, public education, litigation and publications.
Budget: $2,500,000
Employees: Full-time: 85; Part-time: 30; Volunteers: 30; Interns: willing to accept applications

COMMON CAUSE
2030 M Street NW
Washington, DC 20036
Tel. 202/833-1200

Purpose: To improve the way government operates.
Activity: Lobbying.
Budget: $11,600,000
Employees: Full-time: 60; Volunteers: 75; Interns: varies

CONGRESS WATCH
215 Pennsylvania Avenue SE
Washington, DC 20003
Tel. 202/546-4996

Purpose: To represent the public through lobbying Congress, organizing, research and publications.
Activity: Research, lobbying, community organizing and public education.
Budget: $700,000
Employees: Full-time: 22 Part-time: 1; Volunteers: varies; Interns: varies

DEMOCRATIC SOCIALISTS OF AMERICA
180 Varick Street
12th Floor
New York, NY 10014
Tel. 212/962-0390

Purpose: To attain a social order based on popular control of resources and production, economic planning, equitable distribution, feminism, racial equality and non-oppressive relationships.
Activity: Community organizing, publications, public education, research and direct action.
Budget: $500,000
Employees: Full-time: 5; Interns: 3

FRIENDS COMMITTEE ON
NATIONAL LEGISLATION
245 Second Street NE
Washington, DC 20002
Tel. 202/547-6000

Purpose: To bring Quaker values to bear on public policy—especially in the areas of world peace, equity and justice for all, civil rights, environmental quality and economic justice.
Activity: Lobbying, research, education and publications.
Budget: $1,000,000
Employees: Full-time: 18; Part-time: varies; Volunteers: varies; Interns: 4

INSTITUTE FOR POLICY STUDIES
1601 Connecticut Avenue NW, Suite 500
Washington, DC 20009
Tel. 202/234-9382

Purpose: To provide research and public education on economics, politics, culture and social issues of democracy.
Activity: Research, public education and publications.
Budget: $1,900,000
Employees: Full-time: 28; Volunteers: 2; Interns: 15

LEAGUE OF WOMEN VOTERS
1730 M Street NW
Washington, DC 20036
Tel. 202/429-1965

Purpose: To encourage the informed and active participation of citizens in government and influence public policy through education and advocacy.
Activity: Research, lobbying, litigation, publications, direct action, public education, training and technical assistance.
Budget: $3,550,000.
Employees: 50; Part-time: varies; Volunteers: varies; Interns 2

MASSACHUSETTS PUBLIC INTEREST
RESEARCH GROUP
29 Temple Place
Boston, MA 02111
Tel. 617/292-4800

Purpose: To develop policy, coordinate grassroots campaigns, and win legislation to promote environmental preservation, consumer protection, safe

energy and corporate and governmental responsibility.
Activity: Human services, training and technical assistance.
Budget: $4,500,000
Employees: Full-time: 118; Volunteers: 50; Interns: varies

NATIONAL CIVIC LEAGUE
1445 Market Street, Suite 300
Denver, CO 80202-1728
Tel. 303/571-4343

Purpose: To work as a convener to communities interested in collaborative projects to improve the quality of life within their community.
Activity: Training and technical assistance, publications, community organizing and research.
Budget: $2,000,000
Employees: Full-time: 21; Part-time: 1; Interns: 4

NATIONAL WOMEN'S POLITICAL CAUCUS
1275 K Street NW, Suite 750
Washington, DC 20005
Tel. 202/898-1100

Purpose: To increase the number of women elected and appointed to political office.
Activity: Identifies, recruits, trains and supports pro-choice women to run for political office at all levels of government, regardless of party.
Budget: $1,500,000
Employees: Full-time: 15; Volunteers: varies; Interns: varies

NEW YORK PUBLIC INTEREST RESEARCH GROUP, INC.
9 Murray Street
New York, NY 10007-2272
212/349-6460
(Other offices in Buffalo; Syracuse; Cortland; Binghamton, Albany; New Paltz; Purchase; Oswego, Huntington; Stony Brook; Garden City; Old Westbury, and Washington, DC)

Purpose: To advocate for a cleaner environment, consumer protection, fair and open government, mass transit, quality health care, better funding for higher education and other issues of social justice.
Activity: Research, lobbying, student organizing, litigation, publications, community organizing, public education, training and technical assistance.

Budget: $4,000,000
Employees: Full-time: 98; Part-time: varies; Volunteers: varies; Interns: varies

OMB WATCH
1731 Connecticut Avenue NW
4th Floor
Washington, DC 20009-1146
Tel. 202/634-8494

Purpose: To conduct research and support education and advocacy that monitors Executive Branch activities affecting nonprofit, public interest and community groups.
Activity: Research, publications, lobbying, training and technical assistance.
Budget: $550,000
Employees: Full-time: 7; Part-time: varies; Interns: varies

PROJECT VOTE!
1511 K Street NW
Suite 326
Washington, DC 20005
Tel. 202/638-9016

Purpose: To empower low-income and minority individuals by involving them in the democratic process.
Activity: Community organizing, direct action, research, public education, training and technical assistance, lobbying, litigation, human services and publications.
Budget: $1,000,000
Employees: Full-time: 10; Part-time: 2; Volunteers: varies; Interns: varies

THE URBAN INSTITUTE
2100 M Street NW
Washington, DC 20037
Tel. 202/833-7200

Purpose: To conduct research, evaluations, and policy analysis related to the social and economic issues facing the United States (or related issues in developing nations); to improve government decisions and their implementation; and to facilitate informed debate and decision-making by policy-makers.
Activity: Research, publications, training and technical assistance.
Budget: $21,000,000
Employees: Full-time: 200; Part-time: 10; Volunteers: varies; Interns: 10

WISCONSIN CITIZEN ACTION
152 West Wisconsin Avenue, Suite 308
Milwaukee, WI 53203
Tel. 414/272-2562
(Other offices in Madison, Racine/Kenosha,
Eau Claire, and Green Bay)

Purpose: To fight for social and economic justice at local, state and federal levels through issue organizing, grassroots lobbying and electoral action.
Activity: Lobbying, public education, community organizing, research and direct action.
Budget: $1,500,000
Employees: Full-time: 40; Part-time: 3; Volunteers: 5; Interns: varies

8

TOP
TRADE AND
PROFESSIONAL
ASSOCIATIONS

*T*rade and professional associations constitute two of the most important complexes of nonprofit organizations. Formed for a variety of reasons, most of these organizations primarily function to promote the interests of their members. Being nonprofit, cooperative, and voluntary organizations, most of these groups exchange ideas amongst members; examine common professional problems; establish professional standards; engage in technical assistance and community service; and provide mutual assistance. Some of these organizations also do research, provide training, conduct testing, issue certification and awards, offer career assistance, and serve as information clearing-houses for their members. Other associations perform these same functions, but they also are heavily involved in lobbying activities aimed at influencing the content of public policy.

Most trade and professional associations are headquartered in Washington, DC (31%), Chicago (17%), or New York City (14%). The remaining 38% are found in other major metropolitan areas, especially Atlanta, Boston, Cleveland, Minneapolis, Denver, San Francisco, and Los Angeles.

THE ORGANIZATIONS

Similar to the nonprofits in Chapter 7, the organizations identified in this chapter should be treated as a sampler. They by no means represent all associations—only examples of what you will likely encounter once you explore on your own the many thousands of associations found at the international, national, regional, state, and local levels. These groups represent every type of conceivable interest and affiliation, and then some!

While we only describe a few trade and professional associations, you'll discover thousands of other associations that represent numer-ous interest and activity categories. To get information on these and other associations, you'll need to conduct your own research using the many useful resources available in your local library, as we outlined in Chapter 5.

We've chosen to include only trade and professional associations because of their **linkage capabilities** vis-a-vis other types of public, private, and nonprofit organizations. From the perspective of job seekers, these associations provide important linkages—or serve as stepping-stones—to other organizations. Members of trade and profes-sional associations represent over 90 percent of all businesses in the United States. Given their educational and public policy focuses, these organizations constantly interact with government, educational institu-tions, and other nonprofit organizations. If you work for one of these organizations, you will be in a good position to make important contacts for future job and career moves into both the public and private sectors as well as into other areas of the nonprofit world.

Most associations are small, operated by 2 to 10 staff members with annual budgets ranging from $300,000 to $1 million. However, over 500 associations, or nearly 7 percent of the total, have annual budgets in excess of $5 million. These organizations have staffs of 50 or more individuals. For your quick reference, we identify the top 500 such associations—by name only—at the end of this chapter.

Therefore, the organizations identified in this chapter represent some of the largest and most politically active associations. These are well organized associations with large staffs and budgets. They offer a wide range of jobs and numerous opportunities for career advancement within and between these organizations.

OPPORTUNITIES

Trade and professional associations offer excellent opportunities for individuals with a variety of skills. Since most associations are heavily involved in education, training, and lobbying activities, they need well educated individuals who have strong communication and organizational skills. They especially need people who can write, speak, plan, organize, maintain liaison, conduct meetings, and train. They operate large publication programs, publishing everything from newsletters and magazines to catalogs and books; conduct seminars and annual meetings; engage in research for members; and provide technical assistance. Associations with staffs of 100 or more, which usually have a $10+ million annual budget, will offer a large number of highly specialized career opportunities.

RESOURCES

Your single best source of information on associations is the *Encyclopedia of Associations* (Gale Research). Published in four volumes, it includes descriptions of nearly 25,000 associations which are classified into 18 major categories:

1. Trade, business, and commercial
2. Environmental and agriculture
3. Legal governmental, public administration, and military
4. Engineering, technological, and natural and social sciences
5. Educational
6. Cultural

7. Social welfare
8. Health and medical
9. Public affairs
10. Fraternal, nationality, and ethnic
11. Religious
12. Veterans', hereditary, and patriotic
13. Hobby and avocational
14. Athletic and sports
15. Labor unions, associations, and federations
16. Chambers of commerce and trade and tourism
18. Greek and non-Greek letter societies, associations, and federations
19. Fan clubs

These directories also are available in two other versions which cover over 50,000 regional, state, and local associations and nearly 13,000 international associations: *Encyclopedia of Associations: Regional, State, and Local Organizations* and *Encyclopedia of Associations: International Organizations*.

Another useful resource for locating professional and trade associations is the *National Trade and Professional Associations* (Columbia Books). This publication offers five useful indexes to associations—alphabetical, subject, geographic, budget, and executive. While not as detailed as the *Encyclopedia of Associations,* the indexes alone are worth your time and effort in examining this publication.

Armed with these resources, you should be able to uncover numerous associations that might have an ideal job for you. Once you identify an interesting association, be sure to follow our previous advice—call to get information on job opportunities and to get a contact name and verify the address.

THE ASSOCIATIONS

The following list of associations covers a large variety of organizations. Taken together, they offer thousands of job opportunities for enterprising job seekers. Examined separately, one or more of these associations may be an excellent "fit" for you. Make a few phone calls and follow-up with letters and resumes and you may soon discover you've uncovered an extremely rewarding job market!

ACADEMY OF MOTION PICTURE
ARTS AND SCIENCES
8949 Wilshire Blvd.
Beverly Hills, CA 90211
Tel. 310/247-3000

Purpose: To promote the interests of motion picture producers, directors, writers, cinematographers, editors, actors, and craftsmen.
Activity: Education, awards.
Budget: N/A ($10,000,000+)
Employees: 100

ADVERTISING COUNCIL
261 Madison Avenue
New York, NY 10016-2303
Tel. 212/922-1500

Purpose: To conduct public service advertising campaigns in a variety of areas—drug abuse prevention, AIDS prevention, teen alcoholism, child abuse, crime prevention, forest fire prevention.
Activity: Research, education, public service awards.
Budget: $12,000,000
Employees: 42

AIRLINE PILOTS ASSOCIATION
INTERNATIONAL
1625 Massachusetts Ave. NW
Washington, DC 20036
Tel. 703/689-2270

Purpose: To represent the labor interests of its 44,000 members. Serves as the collective bargaining agent.
Activity: Research, education, collective bargaining.
Budget: N/A ($15,000,000+)
Employees: 350

AMERICAN ASSOCIATION OF
AIRPORT EXECUTIVES
4212 King Street
Alexandria, VA 22302
Tel. 703/824-0500

Purpose: Promote the interests of airport management personnel and representatives of companies serving the civil airport industry.

Activity: Education, research, testing.
Budget: $4,100,000
Staff: 25

AMERICAN ASSOCIATION OF RETIRED PERSONS (AARP)
601 E Street NW
Washington, DC 20049
Tel. 202/434-2277

Purpose: To promote the interests of persons 50 years of age or older. Operates a large number of programs, from preretirement planning to group health insurance.
Activity: Education, research, community service, lobbying.
Budget: N/A ($200,000,000+)
Staff: 1,200

AMERICAN AUTOMOBILE ASSOCIATION
1000 AAA Drive
Heathrow, FL 32746
Tel. 407/444-7000

Purpose: To sponsor public services relating to traffic, safety, better highways, energy conservation, and improved motoring conditions. A federation of 1000 automobile clubs with 33,700,000 members.
Activity: Research, education, membership services, lobbying.
Budget: N/A ($30,000,000+)
Employees: N/A (2000+)

AMERICAN AUTOMOBILE MANUFACTURERS ASSOCIATION
1401 H Street NW
Suite 900
Washington, DC 20005
202/326-5500

Purpose: To monitor, analyze, and respond to federal and state legislative and regulatory initiatives affecting the automotive industry. Sponsored by Chrysler, Ford, and General Motors.
Activity: Research, education, lobbying.
Budget: $30,000,000
Employees: 100

AMERICAN BANKERS ASSOCIATION
1120 Connecticut Avenue NW
Washington, DC 20036
202/663-5000

Purpose: To promote the interests of its members—primarily commercial banks and trust companies representing 90% of the banking industry.
Activity: Education, research, testing.
Budget: $62,000,000
Staff: 470

AMERICAN BAR ASSOCIATION
750 N. Lake Shore Dr.
Chicago, IL 60611
Tel. 312/988-5000

Purpose: To promote the interests of its 375,000 members who are attorneys in good standing with the bar of any state.
Activity: Education, research, public service, lobbying.
Budget: $65,000,000
Staff: 800

AMERICAN CANCER SOCIETY
1599 Clifton Road NE
Atlanta, GA 30329
Tel. 404/320-3333

Purpose: To support education and research in cancer prevention, diagnosis, detection, and treatment. Includes 2.5 million volunteers.
Activity: Education, research, public service.
Budget: N/A ($30,000,000+)
Staff: 390

AMERICAN CHEMICAL SOCIETY
1155 16th Street NW
Washington, DC 20036
Tel. 202/872-4600

Purpose: To support the work and interests of chemists and chemical engineers. A scientific and educational society.
Activity: Education, research, public service, career guidance.
Budget: $250,000,000
Staff: 1,950

AMERICAN COMPENSATION ASSOCIATION
14040 N. Northsight Blvd.
Scottsdale, AZ 85260
Tel. 602/951-9191

Purpose: To promote the interests of managerial, professional, and executive level administrative personnel in business, industry, and government who design, establish, execute, administer, or apply total compensation practices and policies in their organizations.
Activity: Surveys, research, education, certification.
Budget: $13,000,000
Employees: 56

AMERICAN COUNCIL OF LIFE INSURANCE
1001 Pennsylvania Avenue NW
Washington, DC 20004-2599
Tel. 202/624-2000

Purpose: To promote the interests of the life insurance industry and to provide effective government relations.
Activity: Education, research, lobbying.
Budget: $34,000,000
Staff: 246

AMERICAN FEDERATION OF LABOR AND CONGRESS OF INDUSTRIAL ORGANIZATIONS (AFL-CIO)
815 16th Street NW
Washington, DC 20006
Tel. 202/637-5000

Purpose: To represent the interests of members before employers and government. A federation of labor unions consisting of 13,300,000 members with 51 state groups and 620 local groups.
Activity: Education, research, lobbying.
Budget: N/A ($35,000,000+)
Staff: 400

AMERICAN FEDERATION OF STATE, COUNTY, AND MUNICIPAL EMPLOYEES
1625 L Street NW
Washington, DC 20036
Tel. 202/429-1000

Purpose: To represent the interests of its 1.3 million members.
Activity: Education, research, organizing, lobbying.
Budget: N/A ($25,000,000+)
Staff: 270

AMERICAN FEDERATION OF TEACHERS
555 New Jersey Avenue NW
Washington, DC 20001
Tel. 202/879-4400

Purpose: To represent the labor interests of its 850,000 teachers and other educational employees through 2,200 chapters at the state and local levels.
Activity: Education, research, organizing, collective bargaining, lobbying.
Budget: $65,000,000
Staff: N/A (400+)

AMERICAN GAS ASSOCIATION
1515 Wilson Blvd.
Arlington, VA 22209
Tel. 703/841-8400

Purpose: To promote the interests of its 4,175 members—individuals (3,500), U.S. (250), and Canadian (11) distributors (utilities) and transporters (pipeline companies) of natural, manufactured, and liquified gas.
Activity: Research, education, testing, public relations, lobbying.
Budget: N/A ($100,000,000+)
Employees: 415

AMERICAN HOSPITAL ASSOCIATION
1 N. Franklin, Suite 27
Chicago, IL 60606
Tel. 312/422-3000

Purpose: To promote improved health care services.
Activity: Research, education, community service, public relations, lobbying.
Budget: $79,000,000
Employees: 884

AMERICAN HOTEL AND MOTEL ASSOCIATION
1201 New York Ave. NW, Suite 600
Washington, DC 20005-3931
Tel. 202/289-3100

Purpose: To promote the interests of this federation of 50 state and regional hotel associations, representing over 1.4 million rooms.
Activity: Education, research, publicity, lobbying.
Budget: $7,000,000
Staff: 65

AMERICAN INSTITUTE OF CERTIFIED PUBLIC ACCOUNTANTS
1211 Avenue of the Americas
New York, NY 10036-8775
Tel. 212/596-6200

Purpose: To establish auditing and reporting standards, influence the development of financial accounting, and preparing and grading the national Uniform CPA Examination for the state licensing bodies.
Activity: Research, continuing education, surveillance.
Budget: N/A ($50,000,000+)
Employees: 725

AMERICAN INSURANCE ASSOCIATION
1130 Connecticut Ave. NW, Suite 1000
Washington, DC 20036
Tel. 202/828-7100

Purpose: To represent companies providing property and casualty insurance and suretyship. Serves as a clearinghouse of ideas, advice, and technical information.
Activity: Education, research, lobbying.
Budget: $25,000,000
Staff: 140

AMERICAN LIBRARY ASSOCIATION
50 E. Huron Street
Chicago, IL 60611
Tel. 312/944-6780

Purpose: To promote and improve library service and librarianship amongst its 56,800 members who are organized into 57 regional groups.

Activity: Education, research, standardization, career assistance, lobbying.
Budget: $31,597,153
Staff: 275

AMERICAN MEDICAL ASSOCIATION
515 N. State Street
Chicago, IL 60610
Tel. 312/464-5000

Purpose: To improve medical education and practices and disseminate scientific information to members and the public.
Activity: Education, research, standardization, placement, lobbying.
Budget: N/A ($30,000,000+)
Staff: N/A (300+)

AMERICAN PETROLEUM INSTITUTE
1220 L Street NW
Washington, DC 20005
Tel. 202/682-8000

Purpose: To represent the interests of its 300 members—corporations in the petroleum and allied industries.
Activity: Education, research, lobbying.
Budget: $56,000,000
Staff: 400

AMERICAN POSTAL WORKERS UNION
1300 L Street NW
Washington, DC 20005
Tel. 202/842-4200

Purpose: To support the labor interests of its 320,000 postal workers.
Activity: Education, research, collective bargaining.
Budget: N/A ($17,000,000+)
Staff: 200

AMERICAN PSYCHIATRIC ASSOCIATION
1400 K Street NW
Washington, DC 20005
Tel. 202/682-6000

Purpose: To further the study of the nature, treatment, and prevention of mental disorders and formulate programs to meet mental health needs.

Activity: Education, research, program development.
Budget: $25,000,000
Staff: 190

AMERICAN PUBLIC HEALTH ASSOCIATION
1015 15th Street NW
Washington, DC 20005
Tel. 202/789-5600

Purpose: To protect and promote personal, mental, and environmental health. A professional organization of 31,500 physicians, nurses, educators, environmentalists, epidemiologists, social workers, optometrists, podiatrists, dentists, nutritionists, health planners.
Activity: Education, research, standards/procedures, job placement.
Budget: $9,000,000
Staff: 65

AMERICAN SOCIETY FOR TRAINING AND DEVELOPMENT
1640 King Street
Alexandria, VA 22313
Tel. 703/683-8100

Purpose: To promote effective practices amongst its 55,000 members who are engaged in the training and development of business, industry, education, and government employees.
Activity: Education, research, clearinghouse.
Budget: $15,000,000
Staff: 120

AMERICAN SOCIETY OF ASSOCIATION EXECUTIVES
1575 Eye Street NW
Washington, DC 20005
Tel. 202/626-2723

Purpose: To promote the interests of paid executives of national, state, and local trade, professional, and philanthropic associations.
Activity: Education, training, lobbying, certification, career guidance.
Budget: $16,000,000
Staff: 125

AMERICAN SOCIETY OF TRAVEL AGENTS
1101 King Street
Alexandria, VA 22314
Tel. 703/739-2782

Purpose: To promote travel and encourage the use of professional travel agents worldwide. Includes 25,000 members.
Activity: Education, training.
Budget: $11,000,000
Staff: 80

AMERICAN TRUCKING ASSOCIATIONS
2200 Mill Road
Alexandria, VA 22314
Tel. 703/838-1700

Purpose: To promote the interests of its 4,400 members—motor carriers, suppliers, trucking associations, national conferences of trucking companies.
Activity: Education, lobbying.
Budget: $37,000,000
Staff: 298

AMERICAN WATER WORKS ASSOCIATION
6666 W. Quincy Avenue
Denver, CO 80235
Tel. 303/794-7711

Purpose: To develop standards and support research programs in waterworks design, construction, operation, and management for its 54,000 members—water utility managers, superintendents, engineers, chemists, bacteriologists, boards of health, manufacturers of waterworks equipment, government officials and consultants involved in water supply.
Activity: Education, training, career assistance.
Budget: $13,000,000
Staff: 120

ASSOCIATION OF INTERNATIONAL AUTOMOBILE MANUFACTURERS
1001 19th Street North, Suite 1200
Arlington, VA 22209
Tel. 703/525-7788

Purpose: To act as a clearinghouse for information affecting the importation of automobiles and auto equipment into the U.S. and report proposed

regulations by state or federal government to members.
Activity: Research, education, lobbying.
Budget: $5,000,000
Staff: 22

ASSOCIATION OF MANUFACTURING TECHNOLOGY
7901 Westpark Dr.
McLean, VA 22102
Tel. 703/893-2900

Purpose: To promote the interests of its 300 members—makers of power driven machines used in the process of transforming man-made materials into durable goods, including machine tools, assembly machines, inspection and testing machinery, robots, parts loaders, and plastics molding machines.
Activity: Research, education, marketing, lobbying.
Budget: $9,000,000
Staff: 70

CHAMBER OF COMMERCE OF THE U.S.A.
1615 H Street NW
Washington, DC 20062
Tel. 202/659-6000

Purpose: To promote the interests of its 219,200 members, a federation of business organizations and companies whose membership includes chambers of commerce, trade and professional associations, and companies.
Activity: Research, education, community action, clearinghouse, lobbying.
Budget: $70,000,000
Staff: 1,200

CHEMICAL MANUFACTURERS ASSOCIATION
2501 M Street NW
Washington, DC 20037
Tel. 202/887-1100

Purpose: To promote the interests of chemical manufacturers and promote public health and safety.
Activity: Research, education, lobbying.
Budget: $36,000,000
Staff: 280

COSMETIC, TOILETRY, AND FRAGRANCE ASSOCIATION
1101 17th Street NW, Suite 300
Washington, DC 20036
Tel. 202/331-1770

Purpose: To promote the interests of manufacturers and distributors of finished cosmetics, fragrances, and personal care products; suppliers of raw materials and services.
Activity: Education, public service, lobbying.
Budget: $7,000,000
Staff: 50

CREDIT UNION NATIONAL ASSOCIATION
P.O. Box 431
Madison, WI 53701
Tel. 608/231-4000

Purpose: To support more than 90% of all local credit unions in the U.S. with a membership totaling more than 65 million people.
Activity: Membership services, research, education, lobbying.
Budget: $27,000,000
Staff: 185

HEALTH INSURANCE ASSOCIATION OF AMERICA
1025 Connecticut Ave. NW, Suite 1200
Washington, DC 20036
Tel. 202/223-7780

Purpose: To support the interests of commercial health insurers in the states and in Washington, DC.
Activity: Research, education, lobbying.
Budget: $20,000,000
Staff: 150

HELICOPTER ASSOCIATION INTERNATIONAL
1635 Prince Street
Alexandria, VA 22314-2818
Tel. 703/683-4646

Purpose: Promotes the interests of owners, operators, helicopter enthusiasts, and affiliated companies in the civil helicopter industry.

Activity: Education, research.
Budget: $3,000,000
Staff: 24

INFORMATION TECHNOLOGY ASSOCIATION
OF AMERICA
1616 N. Fort Myer Drive
Suite 1300
Arlington, VA 22209
Tel. 703/522-5055

Purpose: To promote the interests of companies offering computer software and services. Improve management methods, develop services, and set standards of performance.
Activity: Education, research, lobbying.
Budget: N/A ($3,000,000+)
Employees: 35

INSTITUTE OF GAS TECHNOLOGY
1700 S. Mount Prospect Rd.
Des Plaines, IL 60018-1804
Tel. 708/768-0500

Purpose: To promote the education and research interests of its sponsoring companies that are engaged in the production, processing, transmission, and distribution of natural gas and related fuels; oil and coal producers; engineering firms; and large energy consumers.
Activity: Education, research.
Budget: $30,000,000
Employees: 300

INSTITUTE OF MANAGEMENT
ACCOUNTANTS
10 Paragon Drive
Montvale, NJ 07645
Tel. 201/573-9000

Purpose: To conduct research on accounting and management uses of accounting.
Activity: Research, education, and technical assistance.
Budget: N/A ($10,000,000+)
Employees: 99

INSTITUTE OF REAL ESTATE
MANAGEMENT
430 N. Michigan Avenue
Chicago, IL 60611-4090
Tel. 312/329-6000

Purpose: To promote the interests of its 10,460 members who are real property and asset managers.
Activity: Research, education, accreditation, career assistance.
Budget: $10,100,000
Employees: 80

INSURANCE INSTITUTE OF AMERICA
720 Providence Road
Malvern, PA 19355-0716
Tel. 215/644-2100

Purpose: To support 18 educational programs for property and liability insurance personnel.
Activity: Research, examination, certification, education.
Budget: N/A ($15,000,000+)
Employees: 150

INTERNATIONAL COUNCIL OF
SHOPPING CENTERS
665 5th Avenue
New York, NY 10022
Tel. 212/421-8181

Purpose: To promote professional standards of performance in the development, construction, financing, leasing, management, and operation of shopping centers for its 25,000 members.
Activity: Research, data gathering, education, training.
Budget: $25,000,000
Employees: 100

INTERNATIONAL DAIRY
FOODS ASSOCIATION
1250 H Street NW, Suite 900
Washington, DC 20005
Tel. 202/296-4250

Purpose: To provide services to three constituent groups—Milk Industry Foundation, National Cheese Institute, and International Ice Cream Associa-

tion. Represents processors and manufacturers.
Activity: Research, education, lobbying.
Budget: N/A ($4,000,000+)
Employees: 40

MOTION PICTURE ASSOCIATION OF AMERICA
1600 Eye Street NW
Washington, DC 20006
Tel. 202/293-1966

Purpose: To promote the interests of its nine members—the principal producers and distributors of motion pictures in the U.S.
Activity: Education, lobbying.
Budget: N/A ($12,000,000+)
Employees: 120

NATIONAL ASSOCIATION OF BROADCASTERS
1771 N Street NW
Washington, DC 20036
Tel. 202/429-5300

Purpose: To support its members who are primarily representatives of radio and television stations and networks.
Activity: Research, education, lobbying, career assistance.
Budget: $27,000,000
Employees: 165

NATIONAL ASSOCIATION OF COUNTIES
440 1st Street NW
8th Floor
Washington, DC 20001
Tel. 202/393-6226

Purpose: To support the work of its members—1,750 elected and appointed county governing officials at the management or policy level.
Activity: Research, education, lobbying.
Budget: $10,000,000
Employees: 70

NATIONAL ASSOCIATION OF MANUFACTURERS
1331 Pennsylvania Ave. NW, Suite 1500 N.
Washington, DC 20004
Tel. 202/637-3000

Purpose: To represent the interests of its 12,500 members who have a direct interests in or relationship to manufacturing.
Activity: Research, education, lobbying.
Budget: $15,000,000
Employees: 180

NATIONAL ASSOCIATION OF REALTORS
430 N. Michigan Avenue
Chicago, IL 60611
Tel. 312/329-8200

Purpose: To promote education, professional standards, and modern techniques in specialized real estate work such as brokerage, appraisal, property management, land development, industrial real estate.
Activity: Research, education, lobbying. Represents 750,000 members.
Budget: $40,000,000
Employees: 350

NATIONAL ASSOCIATION OF SOCIAL WORKERS
750 First St. NE, Suite 700
Washington, DC 20002-4241
Tel. 202/408-8600

Purpose: To create professional standards for social work practice; advocate public policies; and provide numerous membership services.
Activity: Research, education, lobbying.
Budget: $14,500,000
Employees: 200

NATIONAL AUTOMOBILE DEALERS ASSOCIATION
8400 Westpark Drive
McLean, VA 22102
Tel. 703/821-7000

Purpose: To promote the interests of its members—19,000 franchised new car and truck dealers.

Activity: Membership services, lobbying.
Budget: $10,000,000
Employees: 400

NATIONAL COAL ASSOCIATION
1130 17th Street NW
Washington, DC 20036
Tel. 202/463-2625

Purpose: To serve as a liaison between federal government agencies and its members—producers and sellers of coal, equipment suppliers, other energy suppliers, consultants, utility companies, and coal transporters.
Activity: Research, education, lobbying, career assistance.
Budget: $7,000,000
Employees: 55

NATIONAL COUNCIL ON THE AGING
409 3rd Street SW
2nd Floor
Washington, DC 20024
Tel. 202/479-1200

Purpose: To promote the interests of older Americans, with a membership of 8,000 drawn from business, industry, organized labor, health professions, social workers, educators, government agencies.
Activity: Research, education, lobbying, community service.
Budget: N/A ($8,000,000+)
Employees: 100

NATIONAL EDUCATION ASSOCIATION
1201 16th Street NW
Washington, DC 20036
Tel. 202/833-4000

Purpose: To promote the professional interests of its 2,000,000 members—elementary and secondary school teachers, college and university professors, administrators, principals, and counselors.
Activity: Research, education, lobbying.
Budget: $147,500,000
Employees: 600

NATIONAL FOOD PROCESSORS ASSOCIATION
1401 New York Ave. NW, Suite 400
Washington, DC 20005
Tel. 202/639-5900

Purpose: To promote the interests of commercial processors of food products, such as fruit, vegetables, meats, seafood, and canned, frozen, dehydrated, pickled, and other preserved food items.
Activity: Research, education, lobbying.
Budget: $16,000,000
Employees: 185

NATIONAL FUNERAL DIRECTORS ASSOCIATION
11121 W. Oklahoma Ave.
Milwaukee, WI 53227-4096
Tel. 414/541-2500

Purpose: To promote the interests of its members—state funeral directors' associations representing 15,000 members.
Activity: Education, home study, lobbying.
Budget: $7,000,000
Employees: 30

NATIONAL RESTAURANT ASSOCIATION
1200 17th St. NW
Washington, DC 20036
Tel. 202/331-5900

Purpose: To promote the interests of its members—restaurants, cafeterias, clubs, drive-ins, caterers, institutional food services, and others
Activity: Research, training, education, lobbying.
Budget: $16,000,000
Employees: 115

NATIONAL SOCIETY OF PUBLIC ACCOUNTANTS
101 N. Fairfax St.
Alexandria, VA 22314-1574
Tel. 703/549-6400

Purpose: To promote the interests of its 20,000 members who are independent practitioners.

Activity: Research, education, lobbying.
Budget: $3,750,000
Employees: 29

OFFICE PRODUCTS MANUFACTURERS ALLIANCE
301 N. Fairfax St.
Alexandria, VA 22314-2696
Tel. 703/549-9040

Purpose: To promote friendship and cooperation among members and enhance relationships with others in the industry. Formerly (1994) known as the Office Products Manufacturers Association.
Activity: Research, education, lobbying.
Budget: $25,000,000
Employees: N/A (175+)

PORTLAND CEMENT ASSOCIATIONS
5420 Old Orchard Road
Skokie,IL 60077
Tel. 708/966-6200

Purpose: To improve and extend the uses of portland cement and concrete for the benefit of its members—manufacturers and marketers in the U.S. and Canada.
Activity: Market promotion, research, education, lobbying.
Budget: $30,000,000
Employees: 265

PROFESSIONAL SECRETARIES INTERNATIONAL
10502 NW Ambassador Dr.
Kansas City, MO 64195-0404
Tel. 816/891-6600

Purpose: To monitor government activities affecting secretaries, sponsor audiovisual products, and offer group insurance.
Activity: Research, education, lobbying.
Budget: $3,500,000
Employees: 27

PROMOTIONAL PRODUCTS ASSOCIATION INTERNATIONAL
3125 Skyway Circle N.
Irving, TX 75038-3526
Tel. 214/252-0404

Purpose: To supply promotional products such as calendars, imprinted ad specialties, premiums, and executive gifts as well as develop industry contacts in 40 countries.
Activity: Education, training, distribution.
Budget: $6,400,000
Employees: 45

THE RETIRED OFFICERS ASSOCIATION
201 N. Washington Street
Alexandria, VA 22314-2539
Tel. 703/549-2311

Purpose: To promote the interests of retired commissioned or warrant officers in the Army, Navy, Air Force, Marine Corps, Coast Guard, NOAA, and Public Health Service.
Activity: Education, membership services, lobbying.
Budget: $10,000,000
Employees: 80

SECURITIES INDUSTRY ASSOCIATION
120 Broadway
New York, NY 10271
Tel. 212/608-1500

Purpose: To promote the interests of its 753 members—investment bankers, securities underwriters, and dealers in stocks and bonds.
Activity: Education, membership services, lobbying.
Budget: N/A ($8,000,000+)
Employees: 97

TOBACCO INSTITUTE
1875 Eye Street NW, Suite 800
Washington, DC 20006
Tel. 202/457-4800

Purpose: To promote the interests of its 12 members—manufacturers of cigarettes, smoking, and chewing tobacco, and snuff.

Activity: Education, training, lobbying.
Budget: N/A ($10,000,000+)
Employees: 50

UNITED STATES CONFERENCE
OF MAYORS
1620 Eye Street NW
Washington, DC 20006
Tel. 202/293-7330

Purpose: To promote improved municipal government for its 1,050 members/mayors who represent cities with populations of over 30,000.
Activity: Education, technical assistance, lobbying.
Budget: $8,600,000
Employees: 50

UNITED STATES MEAT
EXPORT FEDERATION
600 S. Cherry St., Suite 1000
Denver, CO 80222
Tel. 303/399-7151

Purpose: To promote the interests of its 106 members—meat producers, packers, purveyors, exporters, and processors; livestock breeding associations; and manufacturers of meat industry equipment.
Activity: Education, training, technical assistance.
Budget: $15,000,000
Employees: 106

THE TOP 541

The following associations report annual budgets in excess of $5 million. This usually translates into a staff size of more than 50 individuals per association, representing only 7% of all major associations. The majority of associations have annual budgets under $1 million and staffs of fewer than 10 people. Detailed information on each association is provided in both the *Encyclopedia of Associations* and the *National Trade and Professional Associations,* key directories found in the reference section of most public libraries. While these larger associations provide good job opportunities, do not neglect the under $5 million associations. They offer numerous job opportunities.

Academy of General Dentistry
Academy of Motion Picture Arts and Sciences
Actors' Equity Association
Aerospace Industries Association of America
Air and Waste Management Association
Air-Conditioning and Refrigeration Institute
Air Conditioning Contractors of America
Air Force Association
Air Line Pilots Association, International
Aircraft Owners and Pilots Association
Alliance of American Insurers
Aluminum Association
Amalgamated Clothing and Textile Workers Union
Amalgamated Transit Union
American Academy of Dermatology
American Academy of Family Physicians
American Academy of Neurology
American Academy of Neurology
American Academy of Ophthalmology
American Academy of Orthopedic Surgeons
American Academy of Otolaryngology-Head and Neck Surgery
American Academy of Pediatrics
American Academy of Periodontology
American Academy of Physician Assistants
American Alliance for Health, Physical Education, Recreation and Dance
American Animal Hospital Association
American Arbitration Association
American Association for Cancer Research
American Association Clinical Chemistry
American Association for Respiratory Care
American Association for the Advancement of Science
American Association of Advertising Agencies
American Association of Blood Banks
American Association of Community Colleges
American Association of Critical-Care Nurses
American Association of Homes and Services for the Aging
American Association of Individual Investors
American Association of Museums
American Association of Neurological Surgeons
American Association of Nurse Anesthetists
American Association of Oral and Maxillofacial Surgeons
American Association of Orthodontists
American Association of Petroleum Geologists
American Association of Retired Persons
American Association of School Administrators
American Association of State Colleges and Universities
American Association of State Highway and Transportation Officials
American Astronomical Society
American Automobile Manufacturers Association
American Bankers Association
American Bar Association
American Booksellers Association

American Bureau of Shipping
American Cancer Society
American Ceramic Society
American Chemical Society
American Chiropractic Association
American College of Cardiology
American College of Chest Physicians
American College of Emergency Physicians
American College of Healthcare Executives
American College of Obstetricians and Gynecologists
American College of Physicians
American College of Radiology
American College of Surgeons
American Compensation Association
American Concrete Institute
American Correctional Association
American Council of Life Insurance
American Council on Education
American Counseling Association
American Crop Protection Association
American Defense Preparedness Association
American Dental Associates
American Diabetes Association
American Dietetic Association
American Egg Board
American Electronics Association
American Farm Bureau Federation
American Federation of Labor and Congress of Industrial Organizations
American Federation of Musicians of the United States and Canada
American Federation of State, County, and Municipal Employees
American Federation of Teachers
American Forest and Paper Association
American Gas Association
American Geophysical Union
American Hardware Manufacturers Association
American Health Care Association
American Health Information Management Association
American Heart Association
American Horse Shows Association
American Hospital Association
American Hotel and Motel Association
American Industrial Hygiene Association
American Institute for Chartered Property Casualty Underwriters-Insurance
    Institute of America
American Institute of Aeronautics and Astronautics
American Institute of Architects
American Institute of Certified Public Accountants
American Institute of Chemical Engineers
American Institute of Physics
American Insurance Association
American Iron and Steel Institute
American Kennel Club

American Law Institute
American League of Professional Baseball Clubs
American Library Association
American Lung Association
American Management Association
American Marketing Association
American Mathematical Society
American Meat Institute
American Medical Association
American Meteorological Society
American Mining Congress
American National Standards Institute
American National Soda Ash Corporation
American Nuclear Society
American Nurses Association
American Occupational Therapy Association
American Optometric Association
American Osteopathic Association
American Payroll Association
American Petroleum Institute
American Pharmaceutical Association
American Physical Society
American Physical Therapy Association
American Physiological Society
American Planning Association
American Plastics Council
American Podiatric Medical Association
American Postal Workers Union
American Poultry U.S.A.
American Production and Inventory Control Association
American Psychiatric Association
American Psychological Association
American Public Health Association
American Public Power Association
American Public Transit Association
American Public Works Association
American Radio Relay League
American Sheep Industry Association
American Society for Biochemistry and Molecular Biology
American Society for Engineering Education
American Society for Industrial Security
American Society for Microbiology
American Society for Quality Control
American Society for Testing and Materials
American Society for Training and Development
American Society of Anesthesiologists
American Society of Association Executives
American Society of Civil Engineers
American Society of Clinical Oncology
American Society of Clinical Pathologists
American Society of CLU and ChFC
American Society of Composers, Authors and Publishers

American Society of Consultant Pharmacists
American Society of Health-System Pharmacists
American Society of Heating, Refrigeration and Air-Conditioning Engineers
America Society of Interior Designers
American Society of Internal Medicine
American Society of Landscape Architects
American Society of Mechanical Engineers
American Society of Plastic and Reconstructive Surgeons
American Society of Safety Engineers
American Society of Travel Agents
American Soybean Association
American Speech-Language-Hearing Association
American Stock Exchange
American Trucking Associations
American Urological Association
American Veterinary Medical Association
American Water Works Association
American Welding Society
American Wholesale Marketers Association
AMT—The Association for Manufacturing Technology
Appraisal Institute
ASM International
Associated Builders and Contractors
Associated Credit Bureaus
Associated General Contractors of America
Associated Surplus Dealers
Association for Computing Machinery
Association for Information and Image Management
Association for Supervision and Curriculum Development
Association of American Medical Colleges
Association of American Publishers
Association of American Railroads
Association of Christian Schools International
Association of Flight Attendants
Association of International Automobile Manufacturers
Association of Operating Room Nurses
Association of the United States Army
Association of Trail Lawyers of America
Association of Women's Health, Obstetric, and Neonatal Nurses
ATP Tour
Audit Bureaus of Circulations
Automotive Service Association
Bank Administration Institute
Bank Marketing Association
Blue Cross and Blue Shield Association
BPA International
Brotherhood of Maintenance of Way Employees
Building Officials and Code Administrators International
Building Owners and Managers Association International
Business Products Industry Association
Business Technology Association
Career College Association

Catholic Health Association of the United States
Cellular Telecommunications Industry Association
Chamber of Commerce of the United States of America
Chemical Manufacturers Association
Child Welfare League of America
Chlorine Chemistry Council
Coffee, Sugar, and Cocoa Exchange
College of American Pathologists
Commercial-Investment Real Estate Institute
Communications Workers of America
Construction Specifications Institute
Copper Development Association
Cosmetic, Toiletry and Fragrance Association
Cotton Council International
Council for Advancement and Support of Education
Council for Exceptional Children
Council for Tobacco Research-U.S.A.
Council of Better Business Bureaus
Council of Chief State School Officers
Council on Foundations
Credit Union National Association
Cruise Lines International Association
Cystic Fibrosis Foundation
Direct Marketing Association
Directors Guild of America
Distilled Spirits Council of the U.S.
ECRI
Edison Electric Institute
EDUCOM
Electric Power Research Institute
Electronic Industries Association
Emergency Nurses Association
Employee Relocation Council
Endocrine Society, The
Engineered Wood Association
Environmental Industry Associations
Fabricators and Manufacturers Association International
Family Service America
Farm Credit Council
Federation of American Health Systems
Federation of American Societies for Experimental Biology
Federation of State Medical Boards of the U.S.
Financial Executives Institute
Florists' Transworld Delivery Association
Food Marketing Institute
Gas Research Institute
Gemological Institute of America
Geological Society of America
Glass Packaging Institute
Golf Course Superintendents Association of America
Government Finance Officers Association of the United States and Canada
Graphic Arts Technical Foundation

Grocery Manufacturers of America
Group Health Association of America
Health Industry Manufacturers Association
Health Insurance Association of America
Healthcare Financial Management Association
Healthcare Forum, The
Healthcare Information and Management Systems Society
Hobby Industry Association of America
Holstein Association U.S.A.
Hotel Employees and Restaurant Employees International Union
IEEE Computer Society
Independent Bankers Association of America
Independent Cash Register Dealers Association
Independent Insurance Agents of America
Industrial Fabrics Association International
Institute for Interconnecting and Packaging Electronic Circuits
Institute for International Human Resources
Institute of Electrical and Electronics Engineers
Institute of Food Technologists
Institute of Gas Technology
Institute of Industrial Engineers
Institute of Internal Auditors
Institute of Management Accountants
Institute of Nuclear Power Operations
Institute of Paper Science and Technology
Institute of Real Estate Management
Institute of Scrap Recycling Industries
Insurance Institute for Highway Safety
International Transportation Society of America
International Arabian Horse Association
International Association of Bridge, Structural and Ornamental Iron Workers
International Association of Chiefs of Police
International Association of Fire Fighters
International Association of Machinists and Aerospace Workers
International Brotherhood of Boildermakers, Iron Shipbuilders, Blacksmiths,
    Forgers and Helpers
International Brotherhood of Electrical Workers
International Brotherhood of Painters and Allied Trades
International Brotherhood of Teamsters, AFL-CIO
International City/County Management Association
International Conference of Building Officials
International Copper Association
International Council of Shopping Centers
International Dairy Foods Association
International Facility Management Association
International Foundation of Employee Benefit Plans
International Franchise Association
International Ladies Garment Workers' Union
International Lead Zinc Research Organization
International Longshoreman's Association
International Memory Institute
International Reading Association

International Society for Measurement and Control
International Union of Bricklayers and Allied Craftsmen
International Union of Electronic, Electrical, Salaried Machine, and Furniture
    Workers
International Union of Operating Engineers
International Union, United Automobile, Aerospace and Agricultural Implement
    Workers of America
Interstate Natural Gas Association of America
Investment Company Institute
IRSA—The Association of Quality Clubs
Laborers' International Union of North America
Landscape Nursery Council
Life Office Management Association
LIMRA International
Livestock Marketing Association
Magazine Publishers of America
Mastercard International
Medical Group Management Association
Meeting Professionals International
Million Dollar Round Table
Modern Language Association of America
Mortgage Bankers Association of America
Motion Picture Association of America
Motion Picture Export Association of America
Motor and Equipment Manufacturers Association
NACE International
NARD
National Academy of Sciences
National-American Wholesale Grocers' Association
National Association for Home Care
National Association for the Self-Employed
National Association for the Specialty Food Trade
National Association of Broadcast Employees and Technicians
National Association of Broadcasters
National Association of Chain Drug Stores
National Association of College and University Business Officers
National Association of College Stores
National Association of Convenience Stores
National Association of Counties
National Association of Federal Credit Unions
National Association of Home Builders of the U.S.
National Association of Independent Insurers
National Association of Independent Schools
National Association of Insurance Commissioners
National Association of Letter Carriers
National Association of Life Underwriters
National Association of Manufacturers
National Association of Music Merchants
National Association of Printers and Lithographers
National Association of Professional Insurance Agents
National Association of Purchasing Management
National Association of Realtors

National Association of Retired Federal Employees
National Association of Secondary School Principals
National Association of Securities Dealers
National Association of Social Workers
National Association of State Boards of Accountancy
National Association of State Mental Health Program Directors
National Association of Wholesaler-Distributors
National Automobile Dealers Association
National Basketball Association
National Board of Boiler and Pressure Vessel Inspectors
National Business Aircraft Association
National Cable Television Association
National Cargo Bureau
National Cattlemen's Association
National Coal Association
National Collegiate Athletic Association
National Conference of Catholic Bishops
National Conference of State Legislatures
National Cooperative Business Association
National Cotton Council of America
National Council of Architectural Registration Boards
National Council of Juvenile and Family Court Judges
National Council of State Boards of Nursing
National Council of Teachers of Mathematics
National Council of the Churches of Christ in the U.S.A.
National Council of the Paper Industry for Air and Stream Improvement
National Council on Compensation Insurance
National Council on the Aging
National Court Reporters Association
National Decorating Products Association
National Education Association of the U.S.
National Electrical Contractors Association
National Electrical Manufacturers Association
National Federation of Independent Business
National Fire Protection Association
National Food Processors Association
National Football League
National Funeral Directors Association
National Futures Association
National Governors' Association
National Ground Water Association
National Hockey League
National Industries for the Blind
National Institute of Building Sciences
National Insurance Crime Bureau
National Kidney Foundation
National Kitchen and Bath Association
National League for Nursing
National League of Cities
National Live Stock and Meat Board
National Marine Engineers Beneficial Association/National Maritime Union
  of America

National Multiple Sclerosis Society
National Parks and Conservation Association
National Pork Producers Council
National Potato Promotion Board
National Recreation and Park Association
National Restaurant Association
National Retail Federation
National Retail Hardware Association
National Rifle Association of America
National Roofing Contractors Association
National Rural Electric Cooperative Association
National Rural Letter Carriers' Association
National Rural Water Association
National Safety Council
National School Boards Association
National Shooting Sports Foundation
National Society of Professional Engineers
National Society to Prevent Blindness/Prevent Blindness America
National Soft Drink Association
National Spa and Pool Institute
National Sporting Goods Association
National Telephone Cooperative Association
National Tour Association
National Treasury Employees Union
National Wholesale Druggists' Association
NBFA: Association for Independent Marketers of Business Printing and
    Information Management Systems
New York Academy of Sciences
New York Cotton Exchange
New York Merchantile Exchange
New York Stock Exchange
Newspaper Association of America
Nonprescription Drug Manufacturers Association
Nuclear Energy Institute
Oil, Chemical, and Atomic Workers International Union
Oncology Nursing Society
Optical Society of America
Organization for the Protection and Advancement of Small Telephone Companies
Osborne Association
Pharmaceutical Research and Manufacturers of America
Photo Marketing Association-International
Portland Cement Association
Practicing Law Institute
Preferred Hotels and Resorts Worldwide
Printing Industries of America
Produce Marketing Association
Professional Association of Diving Instructors
Professional Bowlers Association of America
Professional Photographers of America
Promotional Products Association International
Public Relations Society of America
Public Securities Association

Radio Advertising Bureau
Radiological Society of North America
Recording Industry Association of America
Recreation Vehicle Industry Association
Residential Sales Council
Retail, Wholesale and Department Store Union
Retired Officers Association, The
Risk and Insurance Management Society
Robert Morris Associates, the Association of Bank Loan and Credit Officers
Savings and Community Bankers of America
Screen Actors Guild
Securities Industry Association
Semiconductor Equipment and Materials International
Services Employees International Union
Sheet Metal and Air Conditioning Contractors National Association
Sheet Metal Workers' International Association
Smokeless Tobacco Council
Social Science Research Council
Society for Human Resource Management
Society for Industrial and Applied Mathematics
Society for Neuroscience
Society of Actuaries
Society of American Florists
Society of Automotive Engineers
Society of Chartered Property and Casualty Underwriters
Society of Critical Care Medicine
Society of Exploration Geophysicists
Society of Manufacturing Engineers
Society of Nuclear Medicine
Society of Petroleum Engineers
Society of Plastics Engineers
Society of the Plastics Industry
Software Publishers Association
Southern Forest Products Association
Special Interest Group on Computer Graphics
SPIE—International Society for Optical Engineering
Sporting Goods Manufacturers Association
Synthetic Organic Chemical Manufacturers Association
Technical Association of the Pulp and Paper Industry
Telecommunications Industry Association
Television Bureau of Advertising
Telecator—The Personal Communications Industry Association
Tobacco Institute
Transaction Processing Performance Council
Transport Workers Union of America
Transportation Communications International Union
Travel Industry Association of America
Treasury Management Association
U.S.A. Poultry and Egg Export Council
Union of American Hebrew Congregations
United Association of Journeymen and Apprentices of the Plumbing and
    Pipe Fitting Industry of U.S. and Canada

United Brotherhood of Carpenters and Joiners of America
United Dairy Industry Association
United Engineering Trustees
United Food and Commercial Workers International Union
United Mine Workers of America International Union
United Paperworkers International Union
United Rubber, Cork, Linoleum and Plastic Workers of America
United States Conference of Mayors
United States Council for International Business
United States Energy Association
United States Golf Association
United States Meat Export Federation
United States Pharmacopeial Convention
United States Soccer Federation
United States Telephone Association
United States Tennis Association
United States Trotting Association
United States Wheat Association
United Steelworkers of America
Universities Research Association
Urban Land Institute
Video Software Dealers Association
Water Environment Federation
Western Railroad Association
Western Wood Products Association
Wine Institute
Yellow Pages Publishers Association
Young Presidents' Organization

9

A WORLD OF NONPROFITS OPERATING ABROAD

*M*ost of the nonprofits identified in previous chapters operate within the United States. They primarily deal with domestic issues or they represent the interests of American trade and professional organizations. Few venture outside the nation's borders.

If you are interested in pursuing global issues, if you get passionate about helping the poor and unfortunate in Third and Fourth World

201

countries, or if you would love to work, travel, and live abroad, this
may be the most important chapter for you. Here, we identify some
of the major nonprofit organizations that tackle today's most pressing
international problems, from disaster relief to feeding the poor and
hungry. They save children, resettle refugees, help improve food
production, educate the poor, provide needed medical assistance, and
prevent blindness. Most of these organizations are charitable groups.
Many of them, especially religious relief groups, are affiliated with
other American nonprofit organizations.

*Nonprofit organizations are
the true missionaries
in today's world.*

THE NEW MISSIONARIES

Nonprofit organizations offer excellent international job opportunities
for enterprising job seekers. These groups are disproportionately
involved in social and economic development efforts in Third and
Fourth World countries—the poor and the poorest of the poor.

Nonprofit organizations are the true missionaries in today's world.
They feed the hungry; care for women and children; promote
improved health care standards; provide needed medical assistance and
education; improve sanitation; evacuate and resettle refugees; develop
rural water and sanitation systems; promote family planning and pre-
natal care; develop rural lending institutions and cooperatives; assist
in marketing crops; and promote community development efforts.
Feeling passionate and powerless about these issues, many people
would love to work for the international nonprofits that specialize in
these problem areas. These nonprofit organizations are the major
catalysts for change in much of the developing world. They rely
heavily on funding from government agencies, especially the United
States Agency for International Development (USAID), and foundations as well as from their own innovative fundraising efforts.

If you are interested in pursuing an international cause or making a difference in the lives of others, you should seriously consider working for an international nonprofit organization. While most of these organizations pay medium to low salaries, they do provide unique and extremely rewarding opportunities to get involved in solving international problems—opportunities that are largely absent with other types of organizations, except for perhaps the U.S. Peace Corps and specialized agencies of the United Nations.

THE ORGANIZATIONS

Nonprofit international organizations are frequently referred to as Nongovernmental Organizations (NGO's) or Private Voluntary Organizations (PVO's). These groups primarily promote a particular international issue or cause. In contrast to over 700,000 nonprofit organizations operating within the United States, international nonprofits are fewer in number and operate almost solely in the international arena. They span a broad spectrum of issues and causes:

foreign affairs	relief
education	human rights
energy	religion
economic development	rural development
population planning	cultural exchange
food	water resources
social welfare	housing
health	community development
children and youth	

Examples of different types of nonprofit organizations and their diverse missions abound throughout the international arena. Most of these organizations cluster around important health, agricultural, social welfare, and disaster issues that are inadequately dealt with in most poor countries: medical services, population planning, agricultural productivity, environment and resource management, community development, employment generation, refugee resettlement, and natural disaster relief. Nonprofit organizations such as the International Voluntary Service, Catholic Relief Service, and CARE provide similar development services as the U.S. Peace Corps. The Population Council's involvement in family planning and health issues affects all other development issues in Third World countries. The World Affairs Councils function to increase the awareness of Americans concerning international issues. The Council for International Exchange of Scholars (Fulbright-Hays) and Meridian House International focus on promoting educational and cultural exchanges.

The major nonprofit international organizations which hire international specialists for headquarter and field locations and have full-time staffs of at least 20 and an annual budget exceeding $5 million include:

- Africare
- Agricultural Cooperative Development International
- American Friends Service Committee
- American Institute for Free Labor Development
- American Jewish Joint Distribution Committee
- Association for Voluntary Sterilization
- Cooperative for American Relief Everywhere, Inc. (CARE)
- Catholic Medical Mission Board
- Catholic Relief Services
- Christian Children's Fund, Inc.
- Church World Service
- Direct Relief International
- Family Planning International Assistance
- Food for the Hungry
- Foster Parents Plan International
- Heifer Project International
- Holt International Children's Services
- The Institute of Cultural Affairs
- Interchurch Medical Assistance, Inc.
- International Eye Foundation
- International Executive Service Corps
- International Human Assistance Programs, Inc.
- International Planned Parenthood Federation
- International Rescue Committee
- Lutheran World Relief
- MAP International
- Mennonite Economic Development Associates, Inc.
- Overseas Education Fund
- Partnership for Productivity International
- Pathfinder Fund

- People to People Health Foundation, Inc.
- Population Council
- Salvation Army
- Save the Children Federation, Inc.
- United Methodist Committee on Relief
- Volunteers in Technical Assistance (VITA)
- World Concern
- World Relief
- World Vision International

Many of these nonprofit organizations, especially population planning groups but also religious-affiliated organizations, are major recipients of USAID contracts. They work closely with the USAID bureaucracy as well as with many private contracting firms and universities that are also major recipients of USAID funding. As such, they play an important role in the peripheral network of organizations involved in U.S. foreign policy efforts. Many other nonprofit organizations are not linked to the government in this manner. Organizations such as Oxfam America, a noted self-help development and disaster relief organization operating in Africa, Asia, Latin America, and the Caribbean, the Pearl S. Buck Foundation that works with Amerasian children, and numerous religious organizations doing development-related missionary work abroad have their own funding sources.

Most of these nonprofit organizations are headquartered in the United States—primarily Washington, DC, New York City, and a few other east coast cities—but have field operations in many countries throughout Latin America, Africa, and Asia. Most of the job opportunities will be in the field and thus require individuals with technical and linguistic skills along with some international experience.

VOLUNTEER OPPORTUNITIES

You will also find numerous volunteer groups operating in Third World countries. Many of these groups, such as Amigos de las Americas (5618 Star Lane, Houston, TX 77057, Tel. 800/231-7796) and Volunteers for Peace (43 Tiffany Road, Belmont, VT 05730, Tel. 802/259-2759), offer students and others opportunities to work on development projects in Third World countries. Many groups require you to pay for your own transportation, food, and housing—which are often minimal—but they do provide excellent opportunities to participate in international development projects without having to join the U.S. Peace Corps or some other type of organization. If you lack international experience and want to "test the waters" to see if this type of international lifestyle is for you, consider joining a volunteer group for three to six months that would put you in a work situation abroad. You will acquire valuable experience and learn a great deal about the Third World and the network of government agencies, nonprofit organizations, and contracting firms operating abroad—as well as yourself.

USEFUL RESOURCES

When conducting research on international nonprofit organizations, you should examine several directories that identify who's who in the international nonprofit arena:

- *Encyclopedia of Associations*
- *Yearbook of International Organizations*
- *USAID Current Technical Service Contracts and Grants*

The first two publications are found in the reference section of most major libraries. The third item, which is literally a roadmap to nonprofit organizations funded by the federal government, is produced by USAID. It is available directly from the agency: USAID, Support Division, Office of Procurement, Procurement Support Division, 1100 Wilson, 14th Floor, Rosslyn, VA 20523, Tel. 703/875-1270.

Several books on international jobs and careers identify and discuss numerous nonprofit organizations offering job opportunities:

- *The Almanac of International Jobs and Careers*
- *American Jobs Abroad*
- *Careers in International Affairs*
- *Guide to Careers in World Affairs*
- *International Careers*
- *International Jobs*
- *Jobs Worldwide*
- *The Nonprofit's Job Finder*

Three special and hard-to-find directories focus specifically on nonprofit international organizations. These include:

Internet Profiles: Published by Network for International Technical Assistance, P.O. Box 3245, Chapel Hill, NC 27515, Tel. 919/968-8324. This is the "bible" for locating organizations involved in development assistance. Provides detailed information on all development-oriented organizations. Since this directory is currently out of print, you may want to check with a major library to see if they have it in their reference section.

InterAction Member Profiles: Published by InterAction, 1717 Massachusetts Avenue NW, 8th Fl., Washington, DC 20036, Tel. 202/667-8227. Profiles nearly 150 private humanitarian agencies that are members of the American Council for Voluntary International Action, one of the largest and most active groups of nonprofit organizations involved in all forms of development assistance, from health care and refugee aid to child care, environment management, human rights, disaster relief, and community development. $37.50.

Overseas Development Network—Opportunities Catalog: A Guide to Internships, Research and Employment With Development Organizations: Published annually by the Overseas Development Network, 333 Valencia Street, No. 330, San Francisco, CA 94103, Tel. 415/431-4204. Describes over 50 development organizations offering internships, research, and employment opportunities for students. Students interested in alleviating global hunger, disease, and poverty should consider joining this network of campus organizations.

Several organizations provide clearinghouse, job listing, and placement services for individuals interested in working for nonprofit international organizations. Among these are:

InterAction: American Council For Voluntary International Action (1717 Massachusetts Avenue NW, 8th Fl., Washington, DC 20036, Tel. 202/667-8227): Consisting of a coalition of over 100 U.S. private and voluntary international organizations, InterAction provides information and advice on employment with nonprofit international organizations. Members of this organization are some of the largest and most active international nonprofit organizations. One of the best international networks providing useful information on organizations and employment opportunities.

CODEL (Coordination in Development, 79 Madison Ave., New York, NY 10016, Tel. 212/685-2030): Clearinghouse for over 40 church-related agencies working abroad.

PACT (Private Agencies Collaborating Together, 777 U.N. Plaza, New York, NY 10017, Tel. 212/697-6222): Consortium of 19 nonprofit agencies working abroad.

The International Service Agencies: (6000 Executive Blvd., Suite 608, Rockville, MD 29852, Tel. 800/638-8079). A federation of 37 American service organizations involved in disaster relief as well as agricultural development, education, job training, medical care, and refugee assistance.

Intercristo, The Career and Human Resources Specialists (19303 Fremont Avenue North, Seattle, WA 98133, Tel. 800/251-7740 or 206/546-7330): This is a Christian placement network which focuses on job opportunities in mission and ministry organizations, many of which are overseas.

If you are in the field of international health, you are fortunate to have a career-aware professional organization to assist you in locating health organizations and job opportunities. The National Council for International Health (NCIH) promotes international health through numerous educational services and publishes the *International Health News*, *Directory of Health Agencies,* and *U.S. Based Agencies Involved in International Health*. It also publishes job listings: *Monthly Job Vacancy Bulletin*. For information on these publications and their job related services, contact:

> National Council for International Health
> 1701 K Street, NW, Suite 600
> Washington, DC 20036
> Tel. 202/833-5900

If you are interested in international volunteer opportunities, including internships, you will find several useful directories and books to assist you in locating organizations whose missions most meet your interests and needs:

- *Alternatives to the Peace Corps: Gaining Third World Experience*
- *Career Opportunities in International Development in Washington, DC*
- *The Directory of International Internships*
- *Directory of Overseas Summer Jobs*
- *Directory of Volunteer Opportunities*
- *The Directory of Work and Study in Developing Countries*
- *The International Directory of Voluntary Work*
- *The International Directory of Youth Internships*
- *International Internships and Volunteer Programs*
- *Invest Yourself: The Catalogue of Volunteer Opportunities*
- *Jobs Abroad: Over 3,000 Vacancies of Interest to Christians*
- *U.S. Voluntary Organizations and World Affairs*
- *Volunteer! The Comprehensive Guide to Voluntary Service in the U.S. and Abroad*
- *Volunteer Vacations*
- *VolunteerWork*
- *Work, Study, Travel Abroad*
- *Work Your Way Around the World*
- *Working Holidays*

Other organizations can provide information on various types of international experiences, including sponsoring internships and volunteer experiences, that can be useful for developing international skills and experiences. A sample of the many such organizations available include:

World Learning: Formerly known as The Experiment in International Living. This well established organization conducts numerous programs in international education, training, and technical assistance, including homestay programs where participants live with families abroad while learning about the local culture. Contact: World Learning, Kipling Road, Brattleboro, VT 05302, Tel. 802/257-7751.

Association Internationale des Etudiants en Sciences Economiques et Commerciales (AIESEC). This international management organization provides students with training opportunities in international business. Most positions are internships with businesses abroad for periods ranging from 2 to 18 months. Contact: Public Relations Director, AIESEC-U.S., Inc., 135 W. 50th Street, New York, NY 10020, Tel. 212/757-3774.

International Association for the Exchange of Students for Technical Experience (IAESTE). Provides students with technical backgrounds opportunities to work abroad for 2-3 month periods. Contact: IAESTE Trainee Program, c/o Association for International Practical Training, Park View Boulevard, 10480 Little Patuxent Parkway, Columbia, MD 21044, Tel. 410/997-2200.

Volunteers for Peace, Inc. Operates a program that places individuals in work camps at home and abroad. Much of the work involves construction, agricultural, and environmental programs. Contact: Volunteers for Peace, Inc., Tiffany Road, Belmont, VT 05730, Tel. 802/259-2759.

Major job listing information services that provide biweekly or monthly information on job vacancies with nonprofit organizations include:

Community Jobs: The Employment Newspaper For the Non-Profit Sector: As mentioned in Chapter 5, this is a "must" resource for anyone looking for a job with nonprofits. Each monthly issue includes some listings for international nonprofit organizations. Individuals can subscribe by sending $29 for 3 issues or $39 for 6 issues to: Access: Networking in the Public Interest, 9th Floor, 30 Irving Place, New York, NY 10003, Tel. 212/475-1001.

International Career Employment Opportunities: Published biweekly and includes more than 500 current openings in the U.S. and abroad, in foreign affairs, international trade and finance, international development and assistance, foreign languages, international program administration, international educational and exchange programs, including internships. Includes positions with the Federal government, U.S. corporations, nonprofits, and international institutions. Contact: International Employment Opportunities, Rt. 2, Box 305, Stanardsville, VA 22973, Tel. 804/985-6444 or Fax 804/985-6828. Subscriptions for individuals cost $7.95 per issue or $29 for 4 issues, $49 for 8 issues, $69 for 12 issues, $129 for 26 issues, or $229 for 52 issues. Includes money back guarantee.

International Employment Gazette: One of the newest and most comprehensive bi-weekly publications listing more than 400 vacancies in each issue. Includes many jobs in construction and business but also with nonprofit organizations. Offers a custom-designed International Placement Network service for individuals. Contact: International Employment Gazette, 1525 Wade Hampton Blvd., Greenville, SC 29609, Tel. 800/882-9188. $35 for 6 issues; $55 for 12 issues; $95 for 24 issues (1 year).

International Jobs Bulletin: A biweekly publication listing information on hundreds of organizations offering job vacancies overseas. Contact: University Placement Center, Southern Illinois University, Carbondale, IL 62901-4703. $25 for 20 issues.

International Employment Hotline: Monthly listing of job vacancies available worldwide in government, consulting firms, nonprofit organizations, educational institutions, and business. Includes informative articles on the problems, pitfalls, and promises of finding an international job, including useful job search tips. Contact: International Employment Hotline, P.O. Box 3030, Oakton, VA 22124, Tel. 703/620-1972. $39 for 12 issues.

Career Network: A monthly job listing bulletin published by the National Council for International Health, 1701 K Street NW, Suite 600, Washington, DC 20006, Tel. 202/833-5900. Includes jobs for health care professionals only. One of the best networks and resources for finding international jobs in health care. Costs $10 per month or $60 per year for members; $20 per month or $120 per year for nonmembers. The membership fee for joining NCIH is $40 for students and $75 for regular members.

Options: Published by Project Concern, P.O. Box 85322, San Diego, CA 92138, Tel. 619/279-9690. Includes jobs for health care professionals in the U.S., East Asia, the Pacific, Latin America, and Africa.

PDRC Placement Hotline: Published by World Learning, Kipling Road, Brattleboro, VT 03302, Tel. 257-7751, Ext. 258.

Monday Developments: Published by InterAction, 1717 Massachusetts Ave. NW, Suite 801, Washington, DC 20036, Tel. 202/667-8227. Published biweekly (every other Monday), a one-year subscription costs $55.

Modern Language Association Job Information Lists: Published four times a year. 62 Fifth Avenue, New York, NY 10011.

If you are a **Returned Peace Corps Volunteer**, you will want to use the job services available through the Returned Volunteer Services office: Peace Corps, 1990 K Street NW, Room 7660, Washington, DC 20526, Tel. 202/606-3126 or 1-800/424-8580, Ext. 2284. Please do not contact this office unless you are a returned volunteer. This already over-worked office can only provide information and services to its former volunteers and staff members—both long-term and recently separated. If you left Peace Corps 20 years ago, you can still use this service. It has an excellent library of international resources as well as numerous job listings relevant to its volunteers. It also publishes a biweekly job listing bulletin called *HOTLINE: A Bulletin of Opportunities for Returned Peace Corps Volunteers*. You should also request a copy of *International Careers*, a useful directory summarizing major international employers relevant to the interests and skills of ex-Peace Corps Volunteers. It may well be worth your time and effort to visit this center. After all, Washington, DC is located in the heart of hundreds of organizations offering international job opportunities for those interested in pursuing jobs and careers with

nonprofit organizations as well as with consulting firms and educational organizations relevant to the Peace Corps experience. Better still,
many of these organizations are staffed by individuals who are part of
the growing "old boy/girl network" of ex-Peace Corps volunteers who
look favorably toward individuals with Peace Corps experience. Better
still, many nonprofit organizations, consulting firms, and educational
organizations automatically contact this office when they have
impending vacancies.

JOB SEARCH STRATEGIES

Use the same strategies for landing a job with an international
nonprofit organization as you would for any other nonprofit organization. This essentially involves networking, informational interviewing,
and moving your face, name, and resume among key people associated with these organizations at both the staff and board levels. Success
in landing such a job will take time, tenacity, and a positive attitude.
Your best locations for literally "hitting the streets" and "pounding the
pavement" for international nonprofit organizations will be Washington, DC and New York City.

Indeed, many international nonprofit organizations are headquartered in the United States, especially New York City and Washington,
DC, but many of them maintain substantial field operations in
developing countries. While most nonprofits hire through headquarters,
many also hire directly in the field. If you are already in the field and
neither have the time nor money to travel to Washington, DC or New
York City to conduct an intensive job search, make sure you develop
contacts with field representatives in your area. Nonprofit organizations tend to be very field oriented and thus many useful job contacts
can be made at the field level. Your research on each organization will
determine how, where, and with whom to best target your job search
within each organization.

INTERNATIONAL NONPROFITS

International nonprofits are modern-day missionaries who are less
motivated by an evangelical zeal to save souls than by a commitment
to humanity—help the very poor move into the mainstream of
development. These organizations appeal to a certain type of person
who still has a missionary zeal to improve the conditions of poor

people throughout the world. They tend to be dedicated to certain human values and committed to helping others. Working conditions for employees of these organizations can be difficult and pay is often low. But these organizations generate a sense of personal satisfaction that cannot always be matched by working for businesses, government, or private contracting firms.

While many of these groups are funded by individual and corporate contributions, most also receive contracts and grants from government agencies and foundations. Some of the more enterprising child survival groups, such as Save the Children Foundation, Foster Parents Plan, Children International, Childreach, and Christian Children's Fund, also operate individual "sponsorship" programs for generating income. You may frequently see their highly effective ads on television which use a variety of major media personalities to solicit for sponsors who pay anywhere from $12 to $22 a month to "sponsor" a child.

NGOs and PVOs are increasingly playing a major role in developing countries. Funding agencies view these groups as most capable of making a difference in developing countries. Their extensive field staffs, commitment to change, and adaptability make them favorite candidates for funding by government agencies and foundations. They continue to expand their operations in Third and Fourth World countries. Consequently, many of these organizations may experience significant growth during the coming decade.

The following international nonprofit organizations are some of the major players in international relief and development. Many are huge organizations with staffs in excess of 1,000 and with annual budgets exceeding $300 million. Some organizations may have 90 percent of their staffs assigned to field operations abroad whereas others may have less than 50 percent stationed abroad. Many of these organizations also operate large volunteer programs.

A few international nonprofits were included in Chapter 7: Accion International, Bread for the World, Greenpeace, Oxfam America, World Resources Institute, World Wildlife Fund, Worldteach, and the Worldwatch Institute. Other groups, such as Planned Parenthood Federation of America with an annual budget over $400 million and a staff of more than 10,000, have large international operations. You may want to review these international nonprofits in reference to the ones identified in this chapter.

ADVENTIST DEVELOPMENT AND
RELIEF AGENCY INTERNATIONAL
12501 Old Columbia Pike
Silver Spring, MD 20904
Tel. 301/680-6380

Purpose: To provide technical assistance in the areas of education, agriculture, health care, nutrition, community development, social welfare, and disaster relief in Africa, Asia, Latin America, and the Pacific region. The development agency of the Seventh Day Adventist Church.
Activity: Education, training, technical assistance.
Budget: $85,000,000
Employees: 92

AFRICARE
440 R Street NW
Washington, DC 20001
Tel. 202/462-3614

Purpose: To provide assistance to Africa in the areas of water resources, agriculture and food production, education, construction, medical care, health services, and refugee assistance.
Activity: Education, technical assistance.
Budget: $13,000,000
Employees: 100

AMERICAN FRIENDS SERVICE COMMITTEE
1501 Cherry Street
Philadelphia, PA 19102
Tel. 215/241-7000

Purpose: To alleviate human suffering and promote global peace. Programs focus on integrated community development, agricultural production, cooperative organization, construction, public health services and refugee assistance. Staff and volunteers operate in 22 countries of Africa, Latin America, the Middle East and Southeast Asia.
Activity: Education, technical assistance.
Budget: $25,000,000
Employees: 356

AMERICAN JEWISH JOINT
DISTRIBUTION COMMITTEE
711 Third Avenue
10th Floor
New York, NY 10017
Tel. 212/687-6200

Purpose: To maintain health, welfare, relief assistance, and rehabilitation programs for needy Jews in over 40 countries in Asia, Africa, Europe, the former Soviet Union, and Latin America.
Activity: Education, community services, technical assistance.
Budget: $90,000,000. Affiliated with the United Jewish Appeal.
Employees: 286

AMERICAN RED CROSS
INTERNATIONAL SERVICES
18th and D Streets NW
Washington, DC 20006
Tel. 202/737-8300

Purpose: To provide relief to disaster victims and refugees and extend assistance in the areas of health care, education, NIV/AIDS education, blood collection and processing, and capacity building. Collaborates with 150 National Red Cross and Red Crescent societies throughout the world. This organization is a part of the larger American Red Cross effort which involves both domestic and international operations.
Activity: Education, technical assistance.
Budget: $1,600,000,000 (American Red Cross National Headquarters)
Staff: 28,323 (American Red Cross National Headquarters)

AMERICARES FOUNDATION
161 Cherry Street
New Canaan, CT 06840
Tel. 203/966-5195

Purpose: To provide international relief by soliciting donations of medicines, medical supplies, and other materials from American companies and delivering them to health and welfare professionals in the U.S. and 39 other countries. Responds to disasters caused by earthquakes, famines, floods, political upheavals, and wars.
Activity: Education, research, technical assistance, airlift/sealift.
Budget: $330,000,000
Employees: 45

CARE
(COOPERATIVE FOR AMERICAN RELIEF EVERYWHERE, INC.)
151 Ellis Street
Atlanta, GA 30303
Tel. 404/681-2552

Purpose: To provide international aid and development assistance by providing food, self-help development, disaster aid, and health carer training overseas. Operates in 39 developing countries in Asia, Africa, and Latin America.
Activity: Emergency relief, technical assistance, education, research.
Budget: $323,357,000
Employees: 8,800

CATHOLIC RELIEF SERVICES
209 W. Fayette Street
Baltimore, MD 21201
Tel. 401/625-2220

Purpose: To conduct programs of disaster response, refugee relief and rehabilitation, social welfare services, and socio-economic development in 67 countries. The nonevangelical overseas relief and self-help development agency of the American Catholic community.
Activity: Disaster relief, education.
Budget: $246,000,000
Employees: 1,600

CHILDREACH
155 Plan Way
Warwick, RI 02886
Tel. 401/738-5600

Purpose: To link caring people in the U.S. with children and their families in developing countries. Conducts one of the most active television and direct-mail campaigns to find "sponsors" for children. U.S. member of PLAN International.
Activity: Sponsorship, education, community development, technical assistance.
Budget: $34,203,961
Employees: 95

CHRISTIAN CHILDREN'S FUND, INC.
2821 Emerywood Parkway
Richmond, VA 23294
Tel. 804/756-2700

Purpose: To provide assistance to needy children and their families in various countries by linking sponsors in the U.S. with children abroad.
Activity: Sponsorship, education, community development, technical assistance.
Budget: $112,000,000
Employees: 200

CHURCH WORLD SERVICE
475 Riverside Drive, Rm. 678
New York, NY 10115-0050
Tel. 212/870-2257

Purpose: To provide worldwide development and emergency aid to the poor in Asia, Africa, Latin America, Middle East, and Eastern Europe. Responds to famines, floods, wars, and other emergencies. Division of the National Council of Churches of Christ.
Activity: Relief, technical assistance, reconstruction.
Budget: $40,000,000
Employees: 170

FOOD FOR THE HUNGRY, INC.
7729 E. Greenway Road
Scottsdale, AZ 85260
Tel. 602/998-3100

Purpose: To extend disaster relief and long-range self-help assistance. To provide information about world hunger, assist with direct relief, and offer developmental assistance in Third World Countries.
Activity: Relief, technical assistance, education.
Budget: $35,000,000
Employees: 42

HELEN KELLER INTERNATIONAL
90 Washington St., 15th Fl.
New York, NY 10006
Tel. 212/943-0890

Purpose: To assist governments and voluntary agencies in Asia, Africa, and the Americas in establishing services to prevent or cure eye diseases and

blindness and to rehabilitate and educate visually disabled persons.
Activity: Education, research, technical assistance, rehabilitation.
Budget: $8,601,000
Employees: 50

INSTITUTE OF INTERNATIONAL EDUCATION
809 United Nations Plaza
New York, NY 10017-580
Tel. 212/883-8200

Purpose: To develop better understanding between the people of the U.S.
and those of other countries through educational exchange programs for
students, scholars, artists, leaders, and specialists. Provides technical
assistance in the area of educational development through the support of
training and education efforts.
Activity: Exchange, education, research, technical assistance.
Budget: $140,000,000
Employees: 350

INTERNATIONAL RESCUE COMMITTEE
386 Park Ave. S., 10th Fl.
New York, NY 10016
Tel. 212/679-0010

Purpose: To assist refugee victims of religious, political, and racial
persecution, civil strife, famine, and war. Operates programs in Africa, Asia,
Central America, Europe, North America, and the Middle East. Founded by
Albert Einstein.
Activity: Relief, education.
Budget: $7,690,536
Employees: 500

INTERNATIONAL RESCUE COMMITTEE
386 Park Ave. S., 10th Fl.
New York, NY 10016
Tel. 212/679-0010

Purpose: To assist refugee victims of religious, political, and racial
persecution, civil strife, famine, and war. Operates programs in Africa, Asia,
Central America, Europe, North America, and the Middle East.
Activity: Relief, education.
Budget: $7,690,536
Employees: 500

LUTHERAN WORLD RELIEF, INC.
390 Park Avenue South
New York, NY 10016
Tel. 212/532-6350

Purpose: To promote integrated community development projects which are usually operated through counterpart church-related agencies in the areas of disaster relief, refugee assistance, and social and economic development.
Activity: Education, research, technical assistance, relief.
Budget: N/A ($40,000,000+)
Employees: N/A (300+)

MAP INTERNATIONAL
2200 Glynco Parkway
P.O. Box 50
Brunswick, GA 31521-0050
Tel. 912/265-6010

Purpose: To help developing countries design, implement, and evaluate community development projects focusing on food production, water resources, health services, nutrition education, and disaster and emergency relief. Works with Christian mission organizations and churches in coordinating programs providing medical supplies, community health developing, and emergency relief.
Activity: Education, training, community development, technical assistance, relief.
Budget: $97,700,000
Employees: 100

MERCY CORPS INTERNATIONAL
3030 SW First Avenue
Portland, OR 97201-4796
Tel. 503/242-1032

Purpose: To provide agricultural development assistance, primary health care, education, and emergency relief services. Motivates and educates the public about the plight of the poor and works for peace and justice.
Activity: Education, training, community development, technical assistance.
Budget: $30,000,000
Employees: 400

PACT
(PRIVATE AGENCIES COLLABORATING TOGETHER)
1901 Pennsylvania Ave. NW, Suite 501
Washington, DC 20006
Tel. 202/466-5666

Purpose: To strengthen the community-focused nonprofit sector worldwide. Identifies and implements participatory development approaches which promote social, economic, political, and environmental justice in the areas of microenterprise development, health care, AIDS treatment and prevention, child welfare, environmental protection, nonformal education, women's issues, and human rights.
Activity: Education, training, technical assistance.
Budget: $20,000,000
Employees: 40

PATHFINDER INTERNATIONAL
9 Galen Street
Suite 217
Watertown, MA 02172-4501
Tel. 617/924-7200

Purpose: To promote population planning through innovative efforts to make fertility services more effective, less expensive, and more readily available to people in developing countries. Improves welfare of families and assists countries in implementing population policies.
Activity: Education, training, technical assistance.
Budget: $50,000,000
Employees: 170

PLAN INTERNATIONAL
155 Plan Way
Warwick, RI 02887
Tel. 401/294-3693

Purpose: To collect and disburse funds raised by 9 national groups, including Childreach (see entry above), for sponsoring children in developing nations of Africa, Asia, and Latin America. Uses funds for promoting self-sustaining communities through education of residents and technical assistance.
Activity: Education, training, technical assistance, sponsorship.
Budget: $175,000,000
Employees: 5,020

POPULATION COUNCIL
1 Dag Hammarskjold Plaza
New York, NY 10017
Tel. 212/339-0500

Purpose: To assist decision makers and population professionals in developing countries to design, implement, and evaluate research and assistance programs. Conducts health and social science programs and research relevant to developing countries; conducts biomedical research to develop and improve contraceptive technology; provides advice and technical assistance to governments, international agencies, and organizations; disseminates information on population issues.
Activity: Education, research, training, technical assistance.
Budget: $46,000,000
Employees: 350

SAVE THE CHILDREN FEDERATION, INC.
54 Wilton Road
Westport, CT 06880
Tel. 203/221-4000

Purpose: To assist children, families, and communities in achieving social and economic stability through community development and family self-help projects in health, education, natural resource management, economic opportunities, and emergency response.
Activity: Education, research, technical assistance, relief.
Budget: $46,000,000
Employees: 350

TECHNOSERVE
49 Day Street
Norwalk, CT 06854
Tel. 203/852-0377

Purpose: To improve the economic and social well-being of low-income people in Latin America, Africa, and Eastern Europe. Helps poor build self-sustaining enterprises.
Activity: Research, technical assistance.
Budget: $9,000,000
Employees: 87

U.S. COMMITTEE FOR UNICEF
333 E. 38th Street
New York, NY 10016
Tel. 212/686-5522

Purpose: To inform U.S. citizens of the U.S. programs of the United Nations Children's Fund and to provide opportunities for American citizens and groups to support its activities and appeals.
Activity: Education, public relations.
Budget: $50,995,000
Employees: 150

VOLUNTEERS IN OVERSEAS COOPERATIVE ASSISTANCE
50 F Street NW
Suite 1075
Washington, DC 20001
Tel. 202/383-4961

Purpose: To recruit and assign volunteers on a short-term basis to provide technical assistance to cooperatives and agricultural producers in developing countries.
Activity: Education, technical assistance.
Budget: $12,000,000
Employees: 150

WINROCK INTERNATIONAL INSTITUTE FOR AGRICULTURAL DEVELOPMENT
Petit Jean Mountain
Route 3, Box 376
Morrilton, AR 72110-9543
Tel. 501/727-5435

Purpose: To alleviate poverty and hunger worldwide through agricultural, rural development, and environmental resources management assistance. Develops farming systems.
Activity: Education, research, technical assistance.
Budget: N/A ($35,000,000+)
Employees: 225

WORLD CONCERN
19303 Fremont Avenue N.
Seattle, WA 98133
Tel. 206/546-7201

Purpose: To empower refugees and poor people through relief and self-help development strategies. Improve health, assist families in attaining self-sufficiency, ensure basic education, prevent diseases, protect livestock, and improve the environment. Christian group.
Activity: Education, technical assistance, community development.
Budget: $21,000,000
Employees: 45

WORLD RELIEF
P.O. Box WRC
Wheaton, IL 60189
Tel. 708/665-0235

Purpose: To provide emergency aid, development assistance, and refugee services in Asia, Africa, Latin America, and the U.S. Conducts programs of disaster relief; refugee relief and resettlement; community development programs, including public health, education, and economic assistance.
Activity: Education, technical assistance, community development.
Budget: $19,000,000
Employees: 297

WORLD VISION
919 W. Huntington Drive
Monrovia, CA 91016
Tel. 818/357-7979

Purpose: To help establish agencies in 94 countries to meet emergency needs, carry out development activities, and provide needed assistance for over 1,000,000 children. Provides food, medicine, education, equipment, personnel, and literature for schools, hospitals, and communities. A Christian relief and development organization.
Activity: Education, technical assistance, community development.
Budget: $250,000,000
Employees: 572

INDEX

SUBJECTS

225

ORGANIZATIONS AND EMPLOYERS

THE
AUTHORS

Ronald L. Krannich, Ph.D. and **Caryl Rae Krannich, Ph.D.** operate Development Concepts Incorporated, a training, consulting, and publishing firm. Ron received his Ph.D. in Political Science from Northern Illinois University. Caryl received her Ph.D. in Speech Communication from Penn State University.

Caryl and Ron are former university professors, high school teachers, management trainers, and consultants. Ron also is a former Peace Corps Volunteer and Fulbright Scholar. Working closely with nonprofit organizations, Ron and Caryl have completed numerous research and technical assistance projects in the United States and abroad on management, career development, local government, population planning, and rural development during the past twenty years. Several of their articles appear in major academic and professional journals.

Authors of 31 career books and 13 travel books, the Krannichs are two of America's leading career and travel writers. Their career books focus on key job search skills, government jobs, international careers, major career fields, and military and civilian career transitions. Their work represents one of today's most extensive and highly praised collections of career writing with such bestsellers as *The Almanac of International Jobs and Careers, The Best Jobs for the 1990s and Into the 21st Century, Change Your Job Change Your Life, Dynamite Answers to Interview Questions, Dynamite Cover Letters, Dynamite Resumes, Dynamite Tele-Search, Find a Federal Job Fast, From Army Green to Corporate Gray, High Impact Resumes and Letters, Interview for Success, Job Search Letters That Get Results,* and *The New Network Your Way to Job and Career Success*. Their books are found in most major bookstores, libraries, and career centers. Many of their works on key job search skills are now available interactively on CD-ROM (*Ultimate Job Source*).

Ron and Caryl continue to pursue their international travel interests through their innovative *Treasures and Pleasures of Exotic Places* travel series. When they are not found at their home and business in Virginia, they are probably somewhere in Hong Kong, China, Thailand, Malaysia, Singapore, Indonesia, Papua New Guinea, Australia, New Zealand, Tahiti, Fiji, Burma, India, Nepal, Morocco, Turkey, Mexico, Italy, France, or the Caribbean pursuing their other passion—shopping and traveling for quality arts and antiques. Most important of all, they're doing what they really love to do, together.

CAREER
RESOURCES

Contact Impact Publications to receive a free copy of their latest comprehensive and annotated catalog of over 1,500 career resources (books, subscriptions, training programs, videos, audiocassettes, computer software, and CD-ROM).

The following career resources, some of which are mentioned in previous chapters, are available directly from Impact Publications. Complete the following form or list the titles, include postage (see formula at the end), enclose payment, and send your order to:

IMPACT PUBLICATIONS
9104-N Manassas Drive
Manassas Park, VA 22111-5211
Tel. 703/361-7300 or Fax 703/335-9486

Orders from individuals must be prepaid by check, moneyorder, Visa MasterCard, or American Express number. We accept telephone and fax orders with a Visa, MasterCard, or American Express number.

Qty.	TITLES	Price	TOTAL
NONPROFITS			
___	Finding a Job in the Nonprofit Sector	$95.00	_____
___	Good Works	$24.95	_____
___	Jobs and Careers With Nonprofit Organizations	$15.95	_____
___	Non-Profits' Job Finder	$16.95	_____
___	Profitable Careers in Nonprofits	$14.95	_____

KEY DIRECTORIES AND REFERENCE WORKS

___ American Salaries and Wages Survey	$115.95	_____
___ Big Book of Minority Opportunities	$39.95	_____
___ Career Training Sourcebook	$24.95	_____
___ Careers Encyclopedia	$39.95	_____
___ Complete Guide for Occupational Exploration	$34.95	_____
___ Consultants and Consulting Organizations Directory	$935.00	_____
___ Dictionary of Occupational Titles	$39.95	_____
___ Directory of Executive Recruiters (annual)	$39.95	_____
___ Encyclopedia of Associations	$1085.00	_____
___ Encyclopedia of Associations: Regional, State, and Local Organizations	$569.00	_____
___ Encyclopedia of Associations: International Organizations	$590.00	_____
___ Encyclopedia of Careers and Vocational Guidance	$129.95	_____
___ Enhanced Guide for Occupational Exploration	$34.95	_____
___ Government Directory of Addresses and Telephone Numbers	$129.95	_____
___ Hoover's Handbook American Business	$29.95	_____
___ Hoover's Handbook World Business	$27.95	_____
___ Job Bank Guide to Employment Services (annual)	$149.95	_____
___ Job Hotlines USA	$24.95	_____
___ Job Hunter's Sourcebook	$69.95	_____
___ Job Seeker's Guide to Private and Public Companies	$389.95	_____
___ Minority Organizations	$49.95	_____
___ National Directory of Addresses & Telephone Numbers	$99.95	_____
___ National Directory of Nonprofit Organizations	$459.95	_____
___ National Job Bank (annual)	$249.95	_____
___ National Trade and Professional Associations	$79.95	_____
___ Occupational Outlook Handbook	$21.95	_____
___ Professional Careers Sourcebook	$89.95	_____
___ Research Center Directory	$495.00	_____
___ Washington Representatives	$99.95	_____

JOB LISTINGS & VACANCY ANNOUNCEMENTS

___ Community (Nonprofit) Jobs (1 year)	$69.00	_____
___ Federal Career Opportunities (6 biweekly issues)	$39.00	_____
___ International Employment Gazette (6 biweekly issues)	$35.00	_____
___ The Search Bulletin (6 issues)	$140.00	_____

INTERNATIONAL JOBS

___ Almanac of International Jobs and Careers	$19.95	_____
___ American Jobs Abroad	$19.95	_____
___ Complete Guide to International Jobs & Careers	$13.95	_____
___ Guide to Careers in World Affairs	$14.95	_____
___ How to Get a Job in Europe	$17.95	_____
___ How to Get a Job in the Pacific Rim	$17.95	_____
___ Jobs for People Who Love Travel	$15.95	_____
___ Jobs in Russia and the Newly Independent States	$15.95	_____
___ Jobs Worldwide	$17.95	_____

GOVERNMENT AND PUBLIC SERVICE JOBS

___ Complete Guide to Public Employment $19.95   _____
___ Directory of Federal Jobs and Employers $21.95   _____
___ Federal Applications That Get Results $23.95   _____
___ Federal Jobs in Law Enforcement $14.95   _____
___ Federal Jobs in Nursing and Health Sciences $14.95   _____
___ Federal Jobs in Office Administration $14.95   _____
___ Federal Jobs in Secret Operations $14.95   _____
___ Find a Federal Job Fast! $13.95   _____
___ Government Job Finder $16.95   _____

ELECTRONIC JOB SEARCH

___ Electronic Job Search Revolution $12.95   _____
___ Electronic Resume Revolution $12.95   _____
___ Electronic Resumes for the New Job Market $11.95   _____
___ Hook Up, Get Hired $12.95   _____
___ Using the Internet in Your Job Search $16.95   _____

CITY AND STATE JOB FINDERS

How to Get a Job in . . .

___ Atlanta $15.95   _____
___ Boston $15.95   _____
___ Chicago $15.95   _____
___ Dallas/Fort Worth $15.95   _____
___ Houston $15.95   _____
___ New York $15.95   _____
___ San Francisco $15.95   _____
___ Seattle/Portland $15.95   _____
___ Southern California $15.95   _____
___ Washington, DC $15.95   _____

Bob Adams' JobBanks to:

___ Atlanta $15.95   _____
___ Boston $15.95   _____
___ Chicago $15.95   _____
___ Dallas/Fort Worth $15.95   _____
___ Denver $15.95   _____
___ Florida $15.95   _____
___ Houston $15.95   _____
___ Los Angeles $15.95   _____
___ Minneapolis $15.95   _____
___ New York $15.95   _____
___ Phoenix $15.95   _____
___ San Francisco $15.95   _____
___ Seattle $15.95   _____
___ Washington, DC $15.95   _____

Job Seekers Sourcebooks to:

___ Boston and New England	$14.95	___
___ Chicago and Illinois	$14.95	___
___ Los Angeles and Southern California	$14.95	___
___ Mid-Atlantic	$14.95	___
___ Mountain States	$14.95	___
___ New York and New Jersey	$14.95	___
___ Northern Great Lakes	$14.95	___
___ Pacific Northwest	$14.95	___
___ Southern States	$14.95	___
___ Southwest	$14.95	___

JOB SEARCH STRATEGIES AND TACTICS

___ 110 Biggest Mistakes Job Hunters Make	$12.95	___
___ Change Your Job, Change Your Life	$15.95	___
___ Complete Job Finder's Guide to the '90s	$13.95	___
___ Dynamite Tele-Search	$12.95	___
___ Five Secrets to Finding a Job	$12.95	___
___ How to Get Interviews From Classified Job Ads	$14.95	___
___ How to Succeed Without a Career Path	$13.95	___
___ Job Hunting After 50	$12.95	___
___ Joyce Lain Kennedy's Career Book	$29.95	___
___ Knock 'Em Dead	$9.95	___
___ Professional's Job Finder	$18.95	___
___ Rites of Passage At $100,000+	$29.95	___
___ Through the Brick Wall	$13.00	___
___ Who's Hiring Who	$9.95	___

BEST JOBS AND EMPLOYERS FOR THE 90s

___ 100 Best Companies to Work for in America	$27.95	___
___ 100 Best Jobs for the 1990s and Beyond	$19.95	___
___ 101 Careers	$17.95	___
___ American Almanac of Jobs and Salaries	$17.00	___
___ America's 50 Fastest Growing Jobs	$9.95	___
___ America's Fastest Growing Employers	$15.95	___
___ Best Jobs for the 1990s and Into the 21st Century	$19.95	___
___ How to Succeed Without a Career Path	$13.95	___
___ Job Seeker's Guide to 1000 Top Employers	$22.95	___
___ Jobs 1995	$15.95	___

ALTERNATIVE JOBS AND CAREERS

___ Adventure Careers	$9.95	___
___ Career Opportunities in the Sports Industry	$27.95	___
___ Career Opportunities in TV, Cable, and Video	$27.95	___
___ Careers for Animal Lovers	$12.95	___
___ Careers for Foreign Language Speakers	$12.95	___
___ Careers for Sports Nuts	$12.95	___
___ Careers for Travel Buffs	$12.95	___

___ Careers in Computers	$16.95	_____
___ Careers in Education	$16.95	_____
___ Careers in Health Care	$16.95	_____
___ Careers in High Tech	$16.95	_____
___ Careers in Medicine	$16.95	_____
___ Environmental Career Guide	$14.95	_____
___ Environmental Jobs for Scientists and Engineers	$14.95	_____
___ New Complete Guide to Environmental Careers	$15.95	_____
___ Nurses and Physicians Career Directory	$17.95	_____
___ Opportunities in Accounting	$13.95	_____
___ Opportunities in Civil Engineering	$13.95	_____
___ Opportunities in Computer Science	$13.95	_____
___ Opportunities in Environmental Careers	$13.95	_____
___ Opportunities in Fitness	$13.95	_____
___ Opportunities in Health & Medical Careers	$13.95	_____
___ Opportunities in Medical Technology	$13.95	_____
___ Opportunities in Microelectronics	$13.95	_____
___ Opportunities in Teaching	$13.95	_____
___ Opportunities in Telecommunications	$13.95	_____
___ Opportunities in Television & Video	$13.95	_____
___ Outdoor Careers	$14.95	_____
___ You Can't Play the Game If You Don't Know the Rules	$15.95	_____

SKILLS, TESTING, SELF-ASSESSMENT, EMPOWERMENT

___ 7 Habits of Highly Effective People	$12.00	_____
___ Discover the Best Jobs for You	$11.95	_____
___ Do What You Are	$14.95	_____
___ Do What You Love, the Money Will Follow	$10.95	_____
___ What Color Is Your Parachute?	$14.95	_____
___ Where Do I Go From Here With My Life?	$10.95	_____
___ Wishcraft	$10.95	_____

RESUMES, LETTERS, & NETWORKING

___ 200 Letters for Job Hunters	$17.95	_____
___ Best Resumes for $70,000+ Executive Jobs	$14.95	_____
___ Dynamite Cover Letters	$11.95	_____
___ Dynamite Resumes	$11.95	_____
___ Electronic Resumes for the New Job Market	$11.95	_____
___ Great Connections	$11.95	_____
___ High Impact Resumes and Letters	$14.95	_____
___ How to Work a Room	$10.95	_____
___ Job Search Letters That Get Results	$15.95	_____
___ New Network Your Way to Job and Career Success	$12.95	_____
___ The Resume Catalog	$15.95	_____
___ Resumes for Re-Entry: A Woman's Handbook	$10.95	_____

DRESS, APPEARANCE, IMAGE

___ 110 Mistakes Working Women: Dressing Smart in the 90s	$9.95	_____
___ John Molloy's New Dress for Success	$13.99	_____

___ Red Socks Don't Work! Messages About Men's Clothing $14.95   _____
___ The Winning Image $17.95   _____

INTERVIEWS & SALARY NEGOTIATIONS

___ 60 Seconds and You're Hired! $9.95   _____
___ Dynamite Answers to Interview Questions $11.95   _____
___ Dynamite Salary Negotiation $12.95   _____
___ Interview for Success $11.95   _____
___ Sweaty Palms $9.95   _____

WOMEN AND SPOUSES

___ Doing It All Isn't Everything $19.95   _____
___ New Relocating Spouse's Guide to Employment $14.95   _____
___ Smart Woman's Guide to Resumes and Job Hunting $10.95   _____
___ Survival Guide for Women $16.95   _____
___ Women's Job Search Handbook $12.95   _____

MINORITIES AND PHYSICALLY CHALLENGED

___ Best Companies for Minorities $12.00   _____
___ Job Strategies for People With Disabilities $14.95   _____

COLLEGE STUDENTS AND GRADUATES

___ 150 Best Companies for Liberal Arts Grads $12.95   _____
___ Graduating to the 9-5 World $11.95   _____

MILITARY TO CIVILIAN TRANSITION

___ Beyond the Uniform $12.95   _____
___ Does Your Resume Wear Combat Boots? $9.95   _____
___ From Air Force Blue to Corporate Gray $17.95   _____
___ From Army Green to Corporate Gray $15.95   _____
___ From Navy Blue to Corporate Gray $17.95   _____

ENTREPRENEURSHIP AND SELF-EMPLOYMENT

___ 101 Best Businesses to Start $16.95   _____
___ Best Home-Based Businesses for the 90s $12.95   _____
___ Entrepreneur's Guide to Starting a Successful Business $16.95   _____
___ Have You Got What It Takes? $12.95   _____
___ How to Start, Run, and Stay in Business $12.95   _____

COMPUTER SOFTWARE

___ FOCIS: Federal Occupational and
     Career Information System $59.95   _____
___ JOBHUNT™ Quick and Easy Employer Contacts $49.95   _____
___ INSTANT™ Job Hunting Letters $39.95   _____
___ ResumeMaker With Career Planner $49.95   _____

CD-ROM

___	America's Top Jobs	$295.00	___
___	Encyclopedia of Associations	$595.00	___
___	Ultimate Job Source	$199.95	___

VIDEOS

___	Dialing for Jobs	$129.00	___
___	How to Present a Professional Image (2 videos)	$149.95	___
___	Insider's Guide to Competitive Interviewing	$59.95	___
___	Networking Your Way to Success	$89.95	___
___	Very Quick Job Search	$129.00	___
___	Winning at Job Hunting in the 90s	$89.95	___

SUBTOTAL ___

Virginia residents add 4½% sales tax ___

POSTAGE/HANDLING ($4.00 for first
title and $1.00 for each additional book) __$4.00__
Number of additional titles x $1.00 ----------- ___

TOTAL ENCLOSED ---------------- ___

SHIP TO:

NAME _____

ADDRESS _____

_____

_____

❏ I enclose check/moneyorder for $ _____ made
payable to IMPACT PUBLICATIONS.

❏ Please charge $ _____ to my credit card:

❏ Visa   ❏ MasterCard   ❏ American Express

Card # _____

Expiration date: _____ / _____

Signature _____

JOBS WITH NONPROFITS KIT

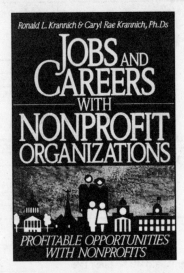

JOBS AND CAREERS WITH NONPROFIT ORGANIZATIONS. *Drs. Ron and Caryl Krannich.* Identifies major nonprofit organizations providing attractive job alternatives: education, public affairs, medical, consumer advocacy, public assistance, charitable, religious, arts, museums, and civil rights. Includes trade and professional associations as well as international groups. Describes major employers, summarizes job strategies, and provides contact information. 256 pages. 1995. $15.95.

NON-PROFIT'S JOB FINDER. *Daniel Lauber.* Shows how to find thousands of jobs with nonprofits by using job hotlines, job matching services, and specialty periodicals with job listings. Includes tips on writing resumes and cover letters and interviewing. 325 pages. 1994. $16.95.

COMMUNITY JOBS. Subscribe to the leading publication on jobs with the nonprofit sector. Each monthly 40+ page issue includes informative articles, book reviews, resource lists, profiles of nonprofits, and over 200 job listings. Includes internships—from entry-level to executive director. Covers all types of organizations including environmental, international, arts, health, civil rights, and human services. $39 for 6 months; $69 for 1 year.

SPECIAL SAVINGS ON TOTAL PACKAGE: Individuals can purchase the complete package (2 books and 6 month subscription) for $69.95. Institutions requiring the 12 month subscription can purchase this package for $99.95. Please add $5.00 shipping for complete package. If ordering individual titles, add $4.00 for first item and $1.00 for each additional item. Send your order to: IMPACT PUBLICATIONS, 9104-N Manassas Drive, Manassas Park, VA 22111 or Fax 703/335-9486 (Visa/MasterCard).
